WEAPON

BROWNING .50-CALIBER MACHINE GUNS

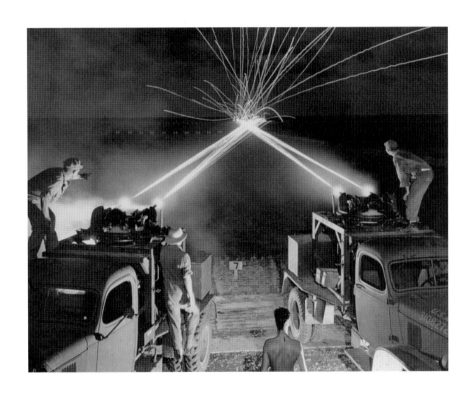

GORDON L. ROTTMAN

Series Editor Martin Pegler

First published in Great Britain in 2010 by Osprey Publishing,
Midland House, West Way, Botley, Oxford, OX2 0PH, UK
44-02 23rd Street, Suite 219, Long Island City, NY 11101, USA

E-mail: info@ospreypublishing.com

© 2010 Osprey Publishing Ltd.

A CIP catalog record for this book is available from the British
Library

Print ISBN: 978 1 84908 330 0

PDF e-book ISBN: 978 1 84908 331 7

Page layout by Ben Salvesen

Index by Alison Worthington

Typeset in Sabon and Univers

Originated by PDQ Digital Media Solutions

Printed in China through World Print Ltd

10 11 12 13 14   10 9 8 7 6 5 4 3 2 1

Osprey Publishing is supporting the Woodland Trust, the UK's
leading woodland conservation charity, by funding the dedication
of trees.

Editor's Note

The following will help in converting measurements referred to in
the text between imperial and metric:

1 mile = 1.6km
1 yard = 0.9m
1ft = 0.3m
1in = 2.54cm/25.4mm

Acknowledgements

The author is indebted to Scott Nye for his invaluable assistance
in regards to .50-caliber ammunition. He is grateful too to the
Texas Military Forces Museum, Austin and the Virginia War
Museum, Norfolk for allowing him to photograph weapons in
their excellent collections.

Glossary

AP	Armor-piercing
API	Armor-piercing incendiary
API-T	Armor-piercing incendiary-tracer
BALL	Standard jacketed, inert ammunition
BOLT	The part of a firearm that closes the breech of the gun for firing, and which usually holds the firing pin; it also often assists feed and extraction
CANNELURE	A knuckled groove in a bullet in which the case mouth is crimped
CHAMBER	The section at the rear of the barrel in which the cartridge is seated prior to firing
COOK-OFF	Caused when a round remains chambered and the overheated barrel and chamber heats the cartridge to the point where the propellant ignites
GROOVES	The spiral incisions cut into the bore of a gun to give the bullet a stabilizing spin. The combination of grooves and lands (q.v.) is called rifling
HANGFIRE	A cartridge that fails to ignite properly on firing, only doing so after a delay
HEADSPACE	The distance between the face of the bolt and the base of the cartridge case when seated in the chamber
HEADSTAMP	The letters, numbers, and symbols marked on the head (base) of a cartridge
LANDS	The sections of the bore between the grooves (q.v.)
OPEN BOLT	A bolt that is held back in the open position (i.e. not closed up to the breech) before firing
RECEIVER	The main body of a gun, containing the major working parts
TIMING	The adjustment of the gun so that firing takes place when the recoiling parts are in the correct position

Cover photograph courtesy US Navy/Kathryn Whittenberger.
Special Warfare Combatant-craft Crewman assigned to Special
Boat Team 22 (SBT-22) reloads an M2HB .50-caliber machine
gun while conducting live-fire immediate action drills at the
riverine training range at Ft Knox. (Top) M2HB photograph
© Cody Images.

Title page image © Joseph Costa/NY Daily News Archive via
Getty Images

CONTENTS

INTRODUCTION

The author's introduction to the "fifty-cal" was the opportunity to fire a few rounds for familiarization during infantry training in 1967. That was after we had been shown the basics of its operation: how to load, cock, fire, and clear it. Such was the extent of our exposure to the legendary "Ma Duce," officially known as "Machine Gun, Caliber .50, Heavy Barrel, M2." The instructor explained that the M2 had been in use since 1933. Some of the trainees, including myself, gazed curiously at the guns placed before us, thinking that they didn't look that old. In fact, the ones we were training with had been manufactured during the Korean War (1950–53). Our introduction to the "fifty" was minimal, as infantrymen did not generally operate the weapon – M2s were typically found in headquarters and support units, mounted on trucks for self-defense, while in mechanized and tank units they were set atop armored fighting vehicles (AFVs). In addition, each self-propelled artillery piece possessed a "fifty."

I discovered more about the .50-cal during subsequent Special Forces training, learning to disassemble the monster and gaining a little more experience in firing it. Yet it was in Vietnam, with some hands-on experience, that I truly learned to appreciate the "Number 50" as the Vietnamese called it. (They also called it the "M50," along the lines of the 7.62mm M60 machine gun.) Observing a US mechanized rifle company "trim the tree line" with a dozen "fifties" made me appreciate that the receiving end of such fire was a place no-one would want to be. Many Special Forces camps had no .50-cals, but others had up to four or more. Ours had two. One was mounted atop a 12ft "Medal of Honor tower," so called because to climb up there during an attack virtually guaranteed you one. The other M2 was atop an inner perimeter bunker. Both were high enough to fire over the barracks on the outer perimeter and into the wire. The tower gun provided 360-degree coverage and the gun on the bunker protected the northern perimeter, the most likely sector to be attacked.

We never actually needed the M2s to defend the camp from human-wave attacks, for which they were originally intended, but they were used for harassing and interdiction on an infiltration trail system a few kilometers from the camp. We liked to think we sometimes made nights more "exciting" for infiltrators tramping down the trails. There was once much consternation from our B-team's S-2 (intelligence officer), after a little Popular Force (local militia) outpost was overrun one night. The Military Assistance Command, Vietnam (MACV) advisors had given them a .50-cal, against the recommendation of our S-2, and it fell into the hands of the Viet Cong (VC). Indeed, the VC goal was not so much to neutralize the outpost, which they successfully did, but to capture the .50-cal. They wanted it bad enough to sacrifice several men. As a result, US/South Vietnamese helicopters in the area had to be more cautious – since among the .50-cal's many varied capabilities, it can be a very effective antiaircraft weapon.

Witnessing the downrange effects of the .50-cal bullet is an eye-opening experience. Bullets punch right through 14in- and 16in-diameter trees, crack through cinderblocks, penetrate two sandbags and foxhole parapets in one go, and hole 1in-thick armor plate, and that was just the standard ball round. There are few who can say they were "wounded" by a .50-cal. Those hit seldom say much more.

Armorers carry six M2 fixed machine guns and their ammunition to a P-51 Mustang fighter. Guns were removed after each mission for thorough inspection, cleaning, and parts replacement. (Cody Images)

Three soldiers of the 62nd Coast Artillery Regiment (Antiaircraft) manning a .50-cal M2 water-cooled gun mounted an M2 antiaircraft mount and fed by a 200-round M2 "tombstone" ammunition chest. A full chest weighed 87lb. (Hulton Archive/Getty Images)

The M2's reliability is also legendary. There are three main causes of .50-cal failure: the operator failing to set the headspace and timing properly after changing the barrel; a part breaks – the M2 is a mechanical device after all, but the parts are so robustly designed that such failure is a rarity; or the gun is hit by enemy fire.[1] It is said that John M. Browning (1855–1926), the gun's designer, produced a freehand drawing of the parts on wrapping paper for his machinist. The machinist asked how thick each portion of the part was and Browning replied by indicating a size between his thumb and forefinger. The machinist measured the distances with calipers and all the parts miraculously fitted together within the receiver's confines as the prototype gun was built.

On the back of this reliability, the Browning .50-cal M2 has become the longest-serving weapon in the US inventory. It first entered service in 1933, is in use today, and it will remain in use for many years to come. Earlier standardized versions date back to 1921 and the prototype itself to 1918. Since then, the M2 has been employed in every imaginable role for a machine gun – antipersonnel, anti-material, light antiarmor, antiaircraft, aboard aircraft as both defensive and offensive armament, as defensive

---

[1] Headspace is the distance between the face of the bolt and the base of the cartridge case when seated in the chamber. Timing is the adjustment of the gun so that firing takes place when the recoiling parts are in the correct position.

armament on armored and soft-skin vehicles, as a ranging gun, and it has been mounted on naval vessels from patrol boats to battleships. In addition, a large number of variants have been developed, discussed in later chapters.

The M2 is considered such an effective and reliable weapon that few countries have ever attempted to develop an equivalent weapon. Instead, it is used worldwide by literally dozens of nations. The British, for example, designated it as the L1A1 and L1A2 12.7mm (.50in) Heavy Machine Gun (HMG) with the Manroy Engineering quick-change barrel, the L111A1, while tank-mounted versions, the L6A1 and L21A1, were used as ranging guns before the advent of laser rangefinders. Before NATO standardization called for metric designations, the British referred to the M2 as the 0.5-inch Browning. In Germany it is known as the MG50-1, Israel as the MAKACH (*Miklah KAliber CHamisheem* = machine gun caliber fifty), Egypt as the DOBSH, Denmark and Norway as the m/50, Netherlands as MIT-12.7, Portugal as the m/55, South Korea as the K6, Sweden as the Tksp 12.7 (*Tung kulspruta* = heavy machine gun), Switzerland as the MG64, Taiwan as the T90, and Thailand as the Pkn. 93. Many countries simply retain the M2 designation. To date, an estimated three million Browning .50-cal machine guns have been made by different producers worldwide and it will be in use for many years, if not decades, into the future. From the aerial dogfights of World War II to the .50-cal-mounted Humvees in Afghanistan at the time of writing, the .50-cal has seen service in virtually every theater and every war since it was first designed.

DEVELOPMENT

The making of a legend

THE NEED FOR A HIGH-POWER MACHINE GUN

The principal development phase of the modern M2 machine gun began in 1918, the last year of World War I, and extended into the early 1930s. In one sense, however, its development story has never really come to an end, as existing models are continuously improved and new variants fielded right up to the present day.

Development of the .50-cal round began in April 1918, when General John J. Pershing requested that a large-caliber machine gun be developed for use against tanks, aircraft, and long-range targets such as far-off enemy artillery crews. Indeed, the cartridge was developed before the gun. The need for such a weapon was first called to the attention of the Ordnance Department by Lieutenant Colonel John H. Parker, the same "Gatling Gun" Parker who as a lieutenant commanded the Gatling Gun Detachment in Cuba in 1898. It was while he was touring a French machine-gun school (rather than commanding a US machine-gun school in France, as is usually reported) that he was introduced to their 11 x 59mmR Gras (.445-cal) Hotchkiss aircraft machine gun.[1] This round provided a more effective incendiary bullet than US .30-cal bullets. Parker was also shown an experimental 12mm (.472-cal) Hotchkiss anti-balloon gun. He obtained one of these guns and shipped it to Frankford Arsenal, Pennsylvania, where he conducted performance testing on the French rounds. Both the 11mm and

---

[1] Metric cartridge designations are often comprised of the approximate caliber in millimeters with the second number being the case length. Rimmed cartridges are further identified by an "R," semi-rimmed rounds by "SR," and belted cartridges (which feature a reinforcing band above the extraction groove) by a "B." Rimless cartridges have no letter identification.

12mm rounds, however, lacked the necessary range and velocity desired by the Army. Pershing, or his ordnance officer, had specified a muzzle velocity of 2,600 feet per second (fps) with a 670-grain bullet. The Army requested that Colt convert eight .30-cal M1917 water-cooled guns to 11mm ammunition for testing, but this configuration proved unsatisfactory.

An alternative route was explored by the firearms manufacturer Winchester. It immediately began work on a new cartridge, a scaled-up .30-cal but with a rim, and referred to as the .50-caliber High Power. At the same time, Winchester was also developing a tripod-mounted, repeating antitank rifle chambered for the cartridge, the bolt-action M1918. The Army preferred a machine gun, however, as both an antiaircraft and a general automatic weapon, the machine gun being perceived as more effective against tanks and long-range targets.

Another discovery of testing with the French ammunition was that the French rimmed 8mm and 11mm rounds were less than ideal for machine-gun belt-feed systems. Consequently, both American Expeditionary Force and Ordnance Department officers felt a rimless round would function better. The prototype was finally developed in June 1918. Yet it was still not firmly established that the new .50-cal would be rimless. Rimless, semi-rimmed, and rimmed cases were all still being tested into the early 1920s, along with scores of different bullet weights and designs, and propellants. Different case lengths were also tested. The 3.89in-long rimless was finally settled on in 1921, but the first officially adopted ball round was not standardized until 1923.

In July 1918, John Browning at Colt had commenced work on scaling up the .30-cal M1917 machine gun to handle the .50-cal rimmed, producing the Colt Mk 50. As a result the water-cooled M1917 can be said to be the father of the .50-cal. Its grandfather was a design Browning had originally developed in 1900, but an actual prototype was not built until 1910, as Browning was preoccupied designing sporting rifles, shotguns, and pistols.

In early 1918, German 13.2 x 92mmSR (.525-cal) antitank rifle cartridges were obtained. This round kicked out a whopping 800-grain steel-cored bullet at 2,750fps, capable of punching through 1in of armor at 250yds. This German round had been originally used in a massive 35lb, 66in-long single-shot, bolt-action, bipod-mounted Mauser antitank rifle called the Tank Abwehr Gewehr Mod. 18 (Tank Defense Rifle Model 18, or T.Gew. – "T-rifle"). The round, often simply called "13mm," was also to be used in a scaled-up Maxim MG08 water-cooled machine gun, the MG18 Tank und Flieger (T.u.F.) Maschinengewehr (MG18 Tank and Aircraft Machine Gun), intended as an antitank and antiaircraft weapon.

A .30-cal Browning M1917. The water-cooled version of the M1917 was said to be the father of the .50-cal, as Browning used a scaled-up version of the .30-cal as the initial basis of his design.

In response to studies of the German round, modifications were made to the US .50-cal round under development, these modifications being conducted in great secrecy – the Ordnance Department did not want it known that German ammunition was considered superior to American. In November 1918, it was decided that further development of the .50-cal round would be undertaken at Frankford Arsenal, although Winchester continued to produce test lots into 1919.

In late 1918, Winchester sent a dummy rimless round to Browning, allowing him to modify the Mk 50 gun from its previous rimmed configuration. Browning took the gun to Winchester for single-shot test firing, to optimize the loading for velocity and reduce the strain on the gun. This cooperation sped up the development process and Browning stayed on at Winchester. In September, the first gun was ready and six more would be built. Six Browning air-cooled .50-cal aircraft guns were also completed, being built by Winchester after modifying Browning's water-cooled design. Browning accomplished the development of the .50-cal machine gun and its ammunition in just over a year, as well as simultaneously handling several other important design projects, including the M1918 Browning Automatic Rifle (BAR), .30-cal M1917 heavy, and M1918 aircraft machine guns.

The first full-automatic test firing of both the water- and air-cooled guns was on November 18, 1918. The newly assembled gun fired about six 100–150-round bursts for a total of 877 rounds at a cyclical rate of 550 rounds per minute (rpm) without a stoppage. The Ordnance Department immediately recommended that 5,000 each of the water- and air-cooled .50-cal M1918 Brownings should be ordered from Winchester. Interestingly, both the T.u.F. MG18 and the US .50-cal M1918 were developed at the same time, both being scaled up from their country's standard rifle-caliber water-cooled machine gun, intended for the same roles, and both were to be fielded in 1919.

John M. Browning himself test fires the first .50-cal water-cooled machine gun in 1918. The gun and tripod were basically a scaled-up .30-cal M1917 Browning, which remained in the Army inventory into the early 1960s. (US Army)

POSTWAR IMPROVEMENTS

The American gun still did not quite meet the US Army's requirements, however. The 707-grain bullet flew at 500fps less than desired by Pershing, only 2,300fps. The prototype guns had only a 30.5in barrel, as this was the longest barrel that Winchester could rifle. An adjusted propellant charge and longer barrel would provide the desired velocity and increase the range. (The .50-cal barrels are rifled with eight lands and grooves with a right-hand twist with one turn in 15in.) Additionally, the infantry found during subsequent trials that the gun was difficult to keep on target, as it rose considerably during firing if not locked in position. But if locked it was almost worthless against moving vehicles, much less aircraft. Moreover its 160lb weight (the weight of the gun with 8qt water and tripod) limited its battlefield mobility, especially in the offense. As an antiarmor, tank-mounted gun, it was also found to be less than optimal. Even Pershing's velocity requirement was insufficient to make it effective against newer tanks, and the bullet was too light. In addition, its rate of fire was too slow for

The first standardized .50-cal Browning was the M1921 water-cooled antiaircraft machine gun with a 36in barrel, here on an M1 AA tripod. It can be seen how the legs hampered the gunner when tracking a high-speed aircraft. It is fitted with a 200-round M2 "tombstone" ammunition case. (US Army)

antipersonnel use, but a higher rate of fire was punishing to the weapon. Just because both the cartridge and weapon were equally scaled-up from their .30-caliber predecessors clearly did not mean that the gun could handle the brutal recoil. The order for the M1918 was cancelled at the war's end, but further development was undertaken to improve the gun and its ammunition.

Browning added several features to the .50-cal gun that were not found on his .30-cal weapons. He included an oil buffer to absorb the action's extensive recoil; it also allowed the rate of fire to be regulated (by reducing the oil flow the rate was reduced). Another innovation was the bolt latch, which held the bolt in the open position when firing ceased. This feature improved cooling, and ensured that the next round was positively chambered when the trigger was pressed to release the bolt and allow it to slam forward. A bar actuated by the trigger allowed the bolt to run positively forward, powered by compression springs. The trigger was operated by thumb pressure. By simply pressing the trigger and immediately releasing it, a single round was fired and the bolt was locked back after recoiling. This allowed single shots to be fired for ranging and then the target engaged with full-automatic fire. If trigger pressure continued to be applied, the gun fired full-automatic. (Browning .30-cal machine guns were full-automatic only, but a good gunner could still snap off single rounds.) Another reason for this single-shot capability was to allow accurate shots to be squeezed off at tanks and other point targets. For a higher degree of control, a pair of spade grips was provided to allow a two-handed grip on the weapon – in comparison, the .30-cal gun only had a single pistol grip.

This prototype M2 gun is mounted on the T21E1 wheeled tripod, which was inadequate for any intended role, whether ground, antiaircraft, or antitank. This gun has a 36in barrel fitted with an experimental T20 muzzle stabilizer, which proved of little use. The gun mounts a T3 telescopic sight, similar to the later M1 sight. (US Army)

Browning continued development of the .50-caliber machine gun and one version was finally adopted: the M1921 water-cooled antiaircraft machine gun, with a secondary antitank role. While type classified (standardized) in 1921, using the M1 antiaircraft tripod, production did not commence until 1926 and then only in limited numbers.

Between 1919 and 1938, ten test guns of various types, as well as 5,757 aircraft guns of different models, 2,475 water-cooled, and 715 air-cooled ground guns, were acquired. The US infantry and cavalry had qualms about the air-cooled guns, however. They were too heavy for manhandling easily and there were difficulties in developing pack mule accommodations. Both arms viewed it first as an antitank weapon and second as an antiaircraft gun. The cavalry had little interest in it as an antiaircraft weapon, preferring to rely on the older .30-cal gun. In the antitank role, they desired as low a cyclical rate as possible – 350–400rpm – quite the opposite of what most users preferred. Indeed, the rpm of the .50-cal was in fact lower than that of the .30-cal (400–500rpm versus 400–550rpm), which made it all but worthless as an antiaircraft gun and not any better for antipersonnel. Both arms tested various mounts and barrel lengths, the cavalry desiring a short barrel for compactness. The cavalry also had a requirement for a longer-barreled air-cooled gun for mounting on scout cars and "combat cars" (a cavalry term for light tanks). The Army Coast Artillery desired the M1921 water-cooled as an antiaircraft weapon, but understood that significant improvements were needed.

No wonder, therefore, that with so many conflicting requirements it was not until 1929 that any procurement headway and any real improvements were made, resulting in the M1921A1 the following year. The most significant alteration was the T5 retracting slide, which made the gun much easier to cock and clear. Rather than just a handle to pull the bolt straight back, this system provided leverage. Minor improvements were also made to the water jacket, water hose connections, rear sight, oil buffer, backplate, trigger, bolt and firing mechanism, and an aluminum muzzle radiator was added, which extended beyond the water jacket. On the M1921A1, the barrel did not extend through the central axis of the water jacket, but was near the bottom as on the .30-cal M1917; more than an inch of muzzle protruded. This overheated rapidly and transferred the heat back down the barrel. The M1921A1 was still a less than desirable weapon, and studies and testing continued.

A 1935 experimental T4 combat car mounted four .30-cal M1919A4 machine guns plus a .50-cal M2 machine gun in the right bow. The gun is fitted with the 36in-long finned barrel. (Cody Images)

ROCK ISLAND ARSENAL
156 RA 946
705-40440 June 27, 1935

The M1921A1 was an interim weapon and did not see wide use, as it was replaced in 1933 after only a few hundred had been made. Some M1921A1s remained in use into World War II, however, used by Army Coast Artillery antiaircraft battalions and Marine defense battalions for close-in air defense, e.g., against fighters and fighter-bombers attacking antiaircraft gun and coast artillery positions.[2] One of the M1921A1's main problems was that the barrel was too short. A longer barrel would provide for a higher velocity, improving range, penetration, and accuracy as well as reducing muzzle flash and smoke. A higher rate of fire would also be more effective against aircraft.

The M1921 water-cooled guns were eventually declared obsolete in 1943, with most having already been converted to M1921A1s. Both were officially declared obsolete on February 15, 1944, and the 51 remaining guns were salvaged for parts and scrapped.

50-caliber M1921 and M1921A1 water-cooled machine guns

	M1921	M1921A1
Gun weight without water	72lb	66lb
Gun weight with water	88lb	79lb
Mount weight (M1 antiaircraft)	191lb	191lb
Overall length	55.9in	55.9in
Barrel length	36in	36in
Rate of fire	500–700rpm	500–650rpm

[2] The Coast Artillery had proponency for Army antiaircraft units from 1917 until it was disbanded in 1950 and absorbed into the Artillery (formerly Field Artillery). Antiaircraft artillery (AAA) units were redesignated air defense (AD) in 1957.

FIGHTING CRITICISM

The US Army Air Corps adopted the M1921 fixed (mounted in wings, fuselages, turrets) and flexible (hand-operated) aircraft guns, with a 500–600rpm rate of fire, on May 30, 1923. Besides the M1921 aircraft guns, there was also an experimental M1922 weapon modified for right-hand feed. The experimental M1923 was convertible to either left- or right-hand feed, and this characteristic would be incorporated into later M2 guns. The Air Corps procured only 990 M1921 aircraft guns between 1925 and 1933.

Most complaints about the .50-cal in fact came from the Air Corps. While many in the service wanted an aircraft gun capable of penetrating armor on future aircraft, and which was able to deliver a large incendiary charge, others opposed the .50-cal. Guns were issued to air units to undertake their own testing, and there were complaints regarding the difficulties of mounting the large, heavy weapons on aircraft and accommodating the ammunition – for every 100 rounds of .50-cal ammunition, 400 rounds of .30-cal could be carried. Aircraft of the era were lightly powered and structurally light. Every pound of extra weight reduced their performance. In ground strafing tests, only 30 percent of the .50-cal rounds hit targets at 500yds and fewer at 1,000yds. The sights were also inadequate at those

The early M2 air-cooled guns had 36in barrels and slots rather than circular holes in the barrel support sleeve. A free-hanging belt, here a white web belt, unsupported by crewmen could jam as the belt's weight was too heavy for the feed mechanism. Stronger belt feed paws were later fitted. (US Army)

ranges. The increased range supposedly offered by the .50-cal was therefore obviated, as the slower rate of fire and sight issues negated the range advantage for pursuit aircraft. Many pilots felt that achieving more hits with .30-cal guns firing at a higher rate (850–1,000rpm) was more effective. It was, however, realized that the .50-cal would be more effective against vehicles, small vessels, and structures than against enemy aircraft. Yet the Air Corps' condemnation of the gun was short-sighted, as more powerful and better-protected aircraft were already under development. Furthermore, the ground targets the US Army Air Forces (USAAF) were later called on to engage in World War II would mainly be vehicles, surface ships, and other hardened targets. Only the Coast Artillery was satisfied with the M1921A1, while the infantry, cavalry, and Air Corps were not. Each branch desired specialized guns and it would be impossible to accommodate all of their requirements in a single weapon.

The US Navy aviation wing's assessment of the .50-cal was in direct contrast to that of the Air Corps. Extensive Navy tests actually found the .50-cal to be more accurate than the Air Corps' locally conducted unscientific tests concluded, and the Navy felt it could be installed in any aircraft mounting. Thus, it was partly the Navy's advocacy and funding that saved the .50-cal machine gun.

DEFINING WEAPONS – THE M2 MACHINE GUNS

A key player in saving the .50-cal machine gun was Dr Samuel G. Green, a Springfield Armory chief engineer. He undertook a study to improve the weapon, which included the ability to convert the gun easily from left- to right-hand feed in the field. (The standard was left-hand feed, but many aircraft and turret installations required right-hand feed.) He redesigned the charging system, strengthened the drive springs, and increased the barrel weight – the latter improved cooling and therefore allowed higher rates of fire. Colt also contributed minor improvements. Green proposed the concept of the "universal" .50-cal machine gun, allowing different barrels and jackets, manual and remote charging systems (cable or air-pressure charging), and changing backplates to accommodate different trigger systems. This approach would also require that mounts and turrets be designed around the gun rather than requiring guns to be built to fit the mount. Another advantage was that trained crewmen could operate any of the guns.

Colt commenced commercial production of the .50-cal for foreign sales in 1924. In 1932, improved Colt commercial models began to be introduced, many of them incorporating the latest military enhancements. These were designated MG52 for water-cooled antiaircraft and MG53 for aircraft guns. Yet through the late 1920s and early 1930s, funding was extremely limited for .50-cal development, and the requirements of different branches were changing and inconsistent. The various improvements resulted in the standardization of the .50-cal T2 as the M1 machine gun in 1932 for infantry and cavalry use. Not a single M1 gun was built, it being placed on standby for production in event of war.

The three .50-cal M2 fixed wing guns of a North American P-51 Mustang fighter. Note the feed chutes leading from the ammunition bins to the guns. The two loose rounds beside the leftmost gun are shown to demonstrate the size. (Courtesy Michael Pereckas)

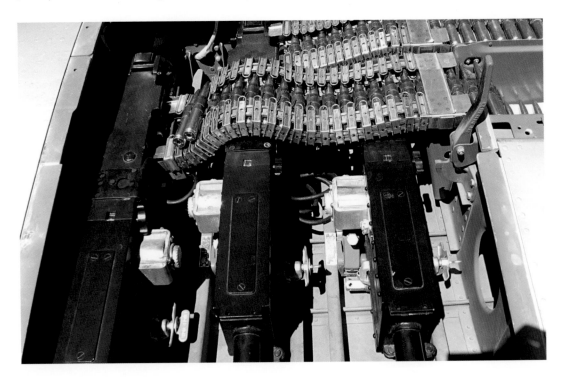

16

Dr Green's proposals were finally accepted on November 16, 1933, and three basic models – water-cooled, air-cooled heavy barrel, and basic aircraft – were standardized, each designated the M2. The basic aircraft model was provided in both fixed and flexible versions and had been previously approved on October 5, 1933, being derived from the M1923. Any one of these guns could be converted to another version by changing the barrel, jacket, and other components. The receiver was the same for all versions; it could be configured for right- or left-hand feed, and the backplate changed to provide a triggerless configuration (without the handgrips plate) for when the backplate, top, or side solenoid triggers were used. Cable, solenoid, and air-pressure charging attachments could replace the retracting charging handle.

On machine guns like the Maxim and Vickers, the barrel jacket and the receiver formed a single component, whether water- or air-cooled. In contrast, each of the three basic M2 guns had its own type of barrel and jacket. The water-cooled gun had a long cylinder jacket containing 2gal of water and fitted with filler/inlet, outlet, and drain plugs. The barrel ran down the center of the jacket to improve cooling and the muzzle did not extend beyond the jacket's front plate. The aircraft guns had lightweight barrels protected by a ventilated full-length sleeve. Early aircraft guns had 16 long ventilating slots in the barrel sleeve, but from *c.* 1940 they had 59 circular holes, which slightly reduced weight and created a stronger sleeve. The air-cooled heavy barrel ground gun had a short 10in-long barrel jacket with 12 slots or 26 holes, the jacket helping to support the comparatively heavy barrel (27.5lb). The heavy barrel allowed higher rates of sustained fire, but slightly reduced the cyclical rate. This version was known as the M2HB or HB, M2.

On the receiver's backplate was the oil buffer tube. This contained screws, retaining ring, spring, and packing material. The tube was necessary to absorb the increased recoil caused by the lighter barrels of the aircraft and water-cooled guns. The M2HB, however, did not need these internal components nor the oil. It was found that guns without the oil buffer tube only increased their firing rate by 40rpm. From the beginning of 1943, these components were removed and not provided in the new M2HB. The housing remained, however, so the gun could be converted to other versions if necessary.

In the years immediately preceding World War II, aircraft design was improving at a rapid rate, with aircraft receiving more armor and being more robustly built. Eventually it was recognized that something more destructive than the .30-cal was needed to arm aircraft, both defensively and offensively. In addition, the Coast Artillery still needed a water-cooled antiaircraft gun, as did the Navy for shipboard use. The M2 supplied the solution to all of these roles. The infantry and cavalry used it as

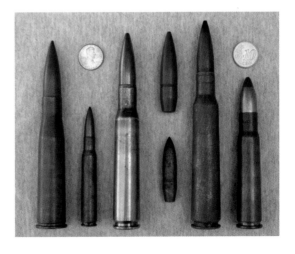

Cartridge size comparison, with (left) US one cent coin, 19.05mm (0.750in) diameter, and (right) ten Euro cent coin, 19.75mm (0.777in) diameter. Cartridges left to right: German 13.2 x 92mmSR AT rifle, which influenced the .50-cal; US .30-06 Springfield, from which the .50-cal was scaled up; US .50-cal (12.7 x 99mm) Browning; .50-cal M33 ball bullet and steel core (10mm diameter); Soviet 12.7 x 107mm API; Italian 12.7 x 81mmSR Breda AP, typical of World War II European 12.7mm and 13.2mm cartridges. (Author's collection)

The waist gun position on the B-24 bomber. The guns are fitted to Mk 6 Mod 3 gun mount adapters. (Cody Images)

a light antitank weapon, both ground- and vehicle-mounted, and it was also mounted on tanks for antiaircraft defense. The Field Artillery used it as a ground- and vehicle-mounted gun for antiaircraft defense as well as against ground targets. Service units mounted the guns on many of their trucks for air defense.

Yet the early M2s still had the 36in barrel. Extensive testing in 1936, however, led to the adoption of a 54in barrel. This barrel improved velocity, range, and accuracy (a 3.5in ten-shot bullet spread, as opposed to 5.25in with the 36in) plus greatly reduced muzzle flash and smoke emissions. The 54in barrel was adopted in 1937 for the ground gun, even though it added significantly to the weapon's weight, and the next year for the water-cooled. However, the Air Corps and Navy aircraft guns retained 36in barrels, as they were more easily accommodated in tight confines. Aircraft guns were issued with four spare barrels owing to their high wear-out rate, due to the light barrel and high rate of fire in action.

There was a fifth M2 version, the Navy Fixed Aircraft (aka "Navy Special"), with a different charging system than the Air Corps M2. The Navy also had a water-cooled version with a 36in barrel and heavier barrel jacket, called the M2A1. This was intended to be fitted on shipboard multiple-gun mounts, but the mounts were never developed. There was also a Navy fixed water-cooled M2, which lacked spade grips. Its production ceased in March 1943 and existing fixed guns were converted to flexible guns.

.50-caliber M2 basic machine guns

	M2HB air-cooled	M2 water-cooled	M2 flexible air-cooled	M2 fixed air-cooled
Gun weight	84lb	100.5lb dry*	68lb	64lb
Overall length	65.13in	65.93in	56in	56.68in
Barrel length	45in	45in	36in	36in
Rate of fire	400–500rpm	500–650rpm	550–650rpm	550–650rpm
	M2HB TT air-cooled	**M2A1 water-cooled†**	**M2 fixed Navy‡**	**AN-M2 fixed**
Gun weight	81lb	94lb dry	66.30lb	61lb
Overall length	65in	57in	54.03in	56.25in
Barrel length	45in	36in	36in	36in
Rate of fire	450–575rpm	500–650rpm	550–650rpm	750–850rpm

* 121.5lb with water

† Navy fixed gun with heavier water jacket

‡ Navy Special fixed aircraft gun

A little-seen version was the M2HB fixed, which was used only on the T52 twin mount fitted in the bow of the never-fielded M6 heavy tank. M2HB guns with solenoid triggers were used as sub-caliber training guns atop tank-destroyer main guns, being fitted with the M9, M10, and M12 sub-caliber mounts. They allowed gunners to practice engaging moving targets on ranges not suited to main gun shooting.

The M2's rear sight was an adjustable leaf sight, graduated from 100 to 2,500yds, and there was a corresponding hooded blade front sight on the forward end of the receiver. The M1 3.25x telescopic sight was developed for use against ground targets, and was graduated from 0 to 3,000yds. (This was a small elbow-type sight and not a long tubular scope.) It saw limited use throughout the war and was declared obsolete at the war's end.

WORLD WAR II: "MEAT CHOPPERS" AND TURRETS

In 1942, the Coast Artillery began to change over from water-cooled M2 guns to air-cooled versions. It was realized that the high speed of ground-attack aircraft drastically reduced engagement time. Only short bursts were possible, and an air-cooled gun could be traversed faster. Another factor was the introduction of the M13 multiple-gun motor carriage in September 1942, with the powered M33 twin-gun turret mounted on the M3 halftrack. Originally the M13 mounted two M2 fixed aircraft guns, each with its barrel and jacket replaced by the heavy barrel and recoil-absorbing Edgewater adapter (for the M33 mount), instead of the short supporting barrel jacket. Navy Mk IX reflector sights were fitted, which were more effective against high-speed aircraft. Some early M15s, which were designed to replace the M13, used water-cooled M2s.

In late 1942, the Ordnance Department recommended the adoption of an additional M2 variant, the M2 Turret Type (TT). Except for the early M33 mount, a special barrel support was used. Multiple guns

Scopes and sights

The M2 guns have attracted many other devices and attachments during and since World War II. Electric gun heaters were clipped onto the gun's receiver when used in high-altitude bombers, to prevent the gun from freezing. Canvas covers were provided for the gun, spare barrel, muzzle, and various mounts. M19 and M20 blank-firing attachments, for example, were adopted in 1980 for the M2 and M85 machine guns respectively. The M3 recoil accelerator, adopted in 1983, is fitted on the M2, allowing plastic training ammunition to be used on reduced-distance ranges. But scopes and sights have been some of the most significant devices developed for use with the .50cal. The 3.25x M1 telescopic sight was used from the late 1930s on M2HBs employed in the antitank role; it was latched onto a dovetail bracket on the right side of the rear leaf sight. It saw very little use during the war and production ceased shortly afterwards. Following the Korean War, the mounting bracket was machined off and new production guns have since lacked the bracket. This step proved shortsighted, for in the early 1960s night-vision devices such as the AN/PVS-2 "starlight scope" were fielded and special mounting brackets were required. In the 1970s, the AN/PVS-20 night-vision sight became available, and it was replaced by the AN/TVS-5 (right) in the late 1970s. The current night sight is the 3.9lb AN/PAS-13(V)3 heavy thermal weapons sight. It can detect the heat signature of targets out to 2,400yds and has a variable magnification of 10x on narrow view and 3.3x on wide view.

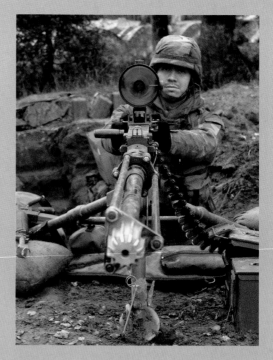

ABOVE

An HB M2 .50-cal machine gun during a field exercise. An AN/TVS-5 Crew-served Night Sight is mounted on the gun and it is fitted with an M19 blank firing attachment. (US Navy/Ronald Gutridge)

compensated for their low 450–550rpm rate of fire, which individually was inadequate for an antiaircraft system. To improve the fire rate, the M45 quad mount was introduced in 1943, becoming known as the "meat chopper" or "Krautmower." While all four barrels could be fired simultaneously, standard practice was to fire only two, alternating between the upper and lower pairs to allow the other pair to cool. This way fire could be sustained for a prolonged period. TT gun production ceased in July 1945. Both the M33 and M45 mounts were developed by the W.L. Maxson Corporation of New York.

The USAAF began phasing out the underpowered .30-cal in August 1942, switching entirely to .50-cals. There was confusion over the definition of fixed and flexible aircraft guns. Fixed guns were for installation in static mountings in aircraft wings, noses, engine cowlings, and other positions. Yet they were also mounted in twin-gun Plexiglas-enclosed turrets and tail positions, in which configuration they were classed as "fixed" in their internal turret mounting. Patrol Torpedo (PT) boats used two fixed twin turret guns, but additional .50-cal flexible aircraft and HB guns were also mounted on PT boats (ranging from one to as many as five) and other

small craft. Fixed guns lacked sights, and were fitted with backplates with solenoid-operated triggers and solenoid, electric, or pneumatic-operated remote charging. Turret gun sights were fitted to the mounting. Flexible guns were fitted with double spade handgrips, butterfly manual triggers, and manual-charging handles. Integral or add-on sights were mainly used aboard bombers in waist, nose, and other positions in which the gunner actually operated the weapon. Among guns installed in aircraft, it was a 50/50 split between right- and left-hand feed guns. While they could be switched from one to the other by armorers, from November 1943 odd serial numbered guns were assembled with right-hand feed and even numbered guns with left-hand.

This M15 multiple-gun carriage mounts two .50-cal M2 water-cooled machine guns plus a 37mm M1A2 automatic gun. Later they more commonly mounted M2 air-cooled guns. Detachable side shields were available, but were often removed to allow the crew more freedom of movement about the gun compartment. (Cody Images)

April 1943: Instructors and students at the Aerial Gunnery School, Harlingen Army Airfield, Texas watch the converging tracers from .50-cal machine-gun turrets mounted on modified 1½-ton cargo trucks. These were used in the ground training phase for aerial gunners. Note the tracks of the ricocheting tracers. (Joseph Costa/NY Daily News Archive via Getty Images)

Throughout the war, numerous modifications were made to correct deficiencies (e.g., when flying upside-down the accelerator might drop and lock the bolt), introduce stronger components, and speed up or simplify manufacture. Regardless of changes in the design of certain parts, they were still interchangeable with earlier weapons and between different manufacturers, even when stampings replaced expensive machined parts. (It is worth noting that more than 4,800 machining procedures, made on 2,000 milling machines, lathes, and other machines were required for a single gun.) Cost was eventually reduced: in 1941 an aircraft gun cost $723, in 1944 just $270. Production quality was also improved. In 1944, Stellite liner inserts were introduced to reduce bore erosion, and extended down the first 7in of the chamber and bore. Chromium-plated bores were introduced later to extend barrel life.

It is a testament to the utility and power of the Browning .50-cal that just prior to the war the Imperial Japanese Army began building copies of the Browning M1921 aircraft machine gun, producing the 50.7lb Type 1 (1941) or Ho-103 (fixed) and Ho-104 (flexible) Kikan-Ho (machine cannon). It did not fire the US 12.7 x 99mm cartridge, but the shorter 12.7 x 81mmSR based on the British Vickers round. The smaller cartridge gave it a 900rpm rate of fire, but only 400rpm if synchronized.

Within 12 hours of Japan's surrender announcement in 1945, telegrams were dispatched to all US manufacturers canceling gun, mount, ammunition, and parts contracts. Additional guns were, however, built during the Korean War. It was planned to contract for more guns during the Vietnam War, but stocks of unused guns were instead discovered in storage and put into action. During both conflicts, older guns were overhauled and worn parts replaced. Nonetheless, several decades later production has now resumed to support operations in Afghanistan and Iraq. The cost of an M2, however, is somewhat greater that that of its World War II-era forefather – a Saco Defense M2HB now costs $14,000.

DEVELOPMENT OF .50-CALIBER M3 AIRCRAFT MACHINE GUNS

In early 1942, US military authorities saw the need for a "high-speed" aircraft machine gun with a much-increased cyclic rate of at least 1,000rpm, plus several other requirements desirable for an aircraft gun. Earlier efforts, such as the M2E1 aircraft gun, had failed to meet such specifications. High Standard began development of the T22 in early 1942 but with no success. This was followed by the T27, which also failed. The later T36 model only increased the rate by 100 rounds, but made other improvements and was adopted as the M2A1 aircraft basic in November 1944. It was canceled after 8,000 were procured. Frigidaire, in the meantime, had made a breakthrough.

The Frigidaire manufacturing contract placed no restrictions on new parts and changes to the gun in order to achieve the desired results. Development of the T25 series began in August 1943, resulting in the T25E3 in July 1944. Its rate of fire eventually reached 1,250rpm. For all practical purposes this weapon was much different when compared to the M2; significantly few parts were interchangeable. But the advent of jet fighters spurred its development. Testing continued and it was standardized as the AN-M3 aircraft machine gun in April 1945. The production of fixed M2 aircraft guns halted in June of that same year and only 3,000 M3s were built before the war's end. Production was resumed during the Korean War and the AN-M3 was mounted in jet fighters such as the F-84 Thunderjet and F-86 Sabre.

The AN-M3 would be phased out in the late 1950s, after being plagued with parts breakages. After testing various .60-cal (15.2 x 114mm) and 20mm revolver and rotary machine guns and cannons, the single-barrel M39 and six-barrel rotary M61 20mm guns were adopted for new jet fighters. Twin-mounted .60-cal T63 machine guns fitted on a M45 mount were tested as antiaircraft weapons, but rejected in 1951.

A new use for the AN-M3 was found in the form of the SUU-12/A gun pod, externally mounted on the Grumman JOV-1A Mohawk armed reconnaissance aircraft. This was a 1960s bomb-shaped pod (pointed at both ends) fitted with an AN-M3 and 750 rounds. The Army used it as the XM14 gun pod on Bell UH-1 Iroquois helicopters.

Troops dismount from a Bell UH-1 Iroquois helicopter during the Vietnam War with protection provided to them by the .50-cal machine guns mounted in the XM14 gun pod. "High-speed" aircraft machine guns were developed during World War II and a generation later the M3 was still in use. (Bettmann/Corbis)

Early B-17 bomber waist positions possessed sliding Plexiglas gun port covers. These were usually removed in combat to provide unlimited gun aiming. The canvas cartridge catch bags were usually discarded. They would fill up too quickly and it required time to remove and dump them. They also added weight to the gun, making it more difficult to traverse. (Cody Images)

FN of Belgium improved the M3 using closer tolerances, heat-treated components, and new alloys. The improved FN M3 can hammer out 600 rounds in a continuous burst without overheating, as opposed to the original AN-M3's 150-round maximum burst. Several versions of the FN guns are still used by the US.

Another new role was found for the AN-M3 as the M3P (Pedestal) air defense machine gun mounted on the AN/TWQ-1 Avenger air defense system, a turret assembly mounting two four-tube Stinger heat-seeking surface-to-air missiles (SAMs), in turn mounted on the M1097 series HMMWV ("Humvee"). The FN-made M3P is mounted on the right side of the turret below the missile pod. It covers the dead zone inside the Stinger's minimum range, and is used against low-performance aircraft

and helicopters. It can also engage ground targets, except those directly to the vehicle's front, which are obscured due to the cab. The gun can be fired from the turret or the driver's station and carries 300 ready rounds. As well as the US Army from 1990, and limited use by the US Marines, the Avenger is used by Egypt, Taiwan, and the United Arab Emirates.

Another FN M3 version is the M3M (Mounted), adopted by the US Air Force, Navy, and Marines as the GAU-21/A in 2004.[3] It replaced the GAU-18/As mounted as door guns in the UH-1, CH-46, CH-53, H-60, and other helicopters. It fires from an open bolt to prevent cook-offs and later versions are fitted with prong-type flash suppressors.[4] The British use the FN M3M helicopter door gun as the L114A1.

A US-made version of the M3 was the General Electric GAU-15/A, used as a door gun in Air Force and Navy helicopters such as the UH-1N, H-46, and H-53. It had a 750rpm rate of fire. The GAU-16/A was a slightly improved version of the GAU-15/A, manufactured by General Electric and used on the UH-1N and SH-60B helicopters.

Ramo Defense Systems, Inc. of Nashville, Tennessee, sells .50-cal machine guns assembled from parts by other manufacturers. One version is the M3R (Ramo) with a variety of trigger and charging systems. The basic gun weighs 61lb, has a 36in barrel, and is 57in long overall. It has a 750–850rpm rate of fire. In the 1980s, Norway required an additional .50-cal gun, so a large number of on-hand AN-M3s were converted to M2 standards as the NM133, for use as vehicle/ground guns.

A Belgian-made .50-cal M3P machine gun mounted on the M1097 Humvee Avenger air defense vehicle. This is provided for use against low-performance aircraft, helicopters, and ground targets. This is in addition to two pods each holding four Stinger heat-seeking missiles. (Cody Images)

[3] Developed under Air Force proponency, "GAU" is an Aeronautical and Support Equipment Type Designation System code and not an abbreviation. "GAU" officially translates to GA = Airborne Gun, U = Unit.
[4] Cook-offs are caused when a round remains chambered and the overheated barrel and chamber heats the cartridge to the point where the propellant detonates. This can result in a "runaway gun," as it begins full-automatic cycling when the round fires regardless of the position of the trigger.

50-caliber M3 machine guns

	AN-M3 aircraft	M3P pedestal	M3M mounted	GAU-21/A
Gun weight	68.75lb	80.25lb	78.9lb	81.57lb
Overall length	57.25in	66.14in*	59.8in	64.8in
Barrel length	36in	35.2in	36in	36in
Rate of fire	1,150–1,250rpm	950–1,250rpm	1,100rpm	950–1,025rpm

* With integral flash suppressor

POST-WORLD WAR II M2 UPGRADES

A variety of M2 upgrades were developed from the 1960s, mainly for use in helicopters and sometimes aboard fixed-wing aircraft. These efforts included reducing weight, increasing the rate of fire, improving reliability, and adapting the guns to fixed and flexible aircraft mountings. Others were improvements of the M2HB ground gun.

The AN-M2 was a postwar version of the fixed aircraft basic gun, with a 36in barrel and higher rate of fire.[5] It replaced the earlier M2 fixed aircraft gun, while the M2 flexible aircraft was phased out since it was no longer mounted in aircraft. The AN-M2 could be mounted on certain antiaircraft mounts, such as the M63 ground and M65 truck pedestal mounts.

The M213 was a much-modified M2 flexible aircraft gun with a ventilated barrel jacket, a built-in recoil damper, and a special muzzle recoil booster to increase the rate of fire. It was mounted on the M59 door pedestal mount, usually on the left side of UH-1D/M helicopters, with a 7.62mm M60 machine gun on the other side. Its rate of fire was 750–800rpm. The M213 was standard for the Army and Marines from 1968 to 1974 when it was made Standard B, being replaced by the XM296. However, only 360 were built.

The GAU-18/A was developed by the US Army as the XM218, a lighter weapon than the M2, and the project was then turned over to the Air Force. It has a lightweight barrel and a 550rpm rate of fire, and is used on pedestal mounts in MH-53J and HH-60 helicopters. The system includes an 850-round ammunition container, but owing to its cumbersome arrangement 100-round cans are often used.

The XM296 was designed in the 1970s as a pod mount for an upgraded M2 machine gun and is still in use. It is a forward-firing weapon mounted on the left side of the OH-58D Kiowa Warrior scout helicopter, fitted with right-hand feed and lacks the single-shot bolt latch. It has a rate of fire of 750–800rpm, but is normally adjusted to 500–650rpm.

General Dynamics Armament and Technical Products offers an M2E2 (not a US Army designation) under the Quick Change Barrel Kit Program, with redesigned barrel changing handle, manual trigger block safety, night-vision sight-friendly flash suppressor, and set headspace and timing.

[5] Often World War II M2 aircraft fixed guns are incorrectly referred to as the "AN-M2," possibly under the assumption that aircraft guns were all designated "AN" owing to the .30-cal AN-M2 and .50-cal AN-M3 aircraft guns. (AN = Army/Navy standardization system.)

An Aviation Warfare Systems Operator, assigned to the "Emerald Knights" Helicopter Anti-Submarine Squadron Seven Five, fires an M3 variant .50-cal machine gun at a target towed alongside the aircraft carrier USS *John F. Kennedy*. The towed target represents a small attack craft, much smaller than the actual craft, which provides a more challenging training target. (US Navy/Tommy Gilligan)

Instead of several minutes for a barrel change, the task can be accomplished in ten seconds. M2E2s have been purchased by Colombia, Egypt, and Saudi Arabia.

Saco Defense Systems produces a lightened M2 known as the Fifty/.50 that incorporates construction techniques and materials that have reduced the weight of the basic gun to 56lb, a 33 percent reduction. Some 72 percent of the parts are interchangeable with the standard M2HB. The rate of fire can be adjusted between 500 and 725rpm.

After World War II, the British modified the US-made M2s by fitting a 36in barrel to make them easier to carry in the field; this is known as the Mk I. British and Belgian parachute units were equipped with this gun. Later the Mk Is were modified to produce the L1A1, still with a 36in barrel, plus modified trigger and operating handle. The L1A2 has a 45in barrel, improved sights, and mount buffering. These are mainly mounted on vehicles for antiaircraft defense, but can be fitted to a variety of ground mounts. In 1996/97 the L1A2 was upgraded with the Manroy quick-change barrel to become the L111A1. Specialized versions of the M2 were used as ranging machine guns: the L6A1 in the 105mm gun-armed Centurion and the L21A1 in the 120mm gun-armed Chieftain tanks, prior to the introduction of laser rangefinders. They were mounted internally and fired in three-round bursts using spotter-tracer ammunition.

A .50-cal M2E2 machine gun includes the Quick Change Barrel Kit Program with redesigned barrel changing handle, manual trigger block safety, night-vision sight-friendly flash suppressor, and set headspace and timing. (Courtesy General Dynamics)

NON-BROWNING .50-CALIBER MACHINE GUNS

Several non-Browning .50-cal weapons have been developed with the intention of supplementing or replacing the M2, but none have met the challenge. In the mid-1950s, for example, the 105mm gun-armed M60 main battle tank was under development. The designers wanted to mount a .50-cal machine gun within a small cupola turret over the commander's hatch. This would allow the commander to operate the gun while protected from small-arms, fragmentation, nuclear, biological, and chemical effects. Yet the M2 required too large a cupola, owing to its receiver length. (M48A1, A2, and A3 tanks had an impossibly cramped M1 cupola mounting a .50-cal M2, and had space for only 50 rounds. In Vietnam the gun was sometimes removed and mounted outside the cupola.) Aircraft Armaments Inc. in Cockeysville, Maryland, therefore developed the T175E2 machine gun to fit inside the M19 cupola, using left-hand feed.

The T175E2 was a lighter and more compact (the receiver was about 8in shorter than the M2's) .50-cal capable of selectable rates of fire for ground and aerial targets, adaptable to left or right feed, and incorporating a quick-change barrel with fixed headspace and an integral flash suppressor. It could be disassembled in 15 seconds, the barrel changed in five seconds, and it could be fired by electric solenoid or manually. For sighting, the M19 cupola was fitted with an 8x telescope, and the gun was charged and fired by pull-chains with color-coded handles (black = charging, red = firing). Internally the recoil-operated gun was also entirely different from the Browning. Adopted as the .50-cal M85 fixed

The M1 Abrams main gun battle tank mounts a .50-cal HB M2 on the commander's cupola and a 7.62mm M240 at the loader's hatch. (Cody Images)

machine gun and built by General Electric, it was fielded in 1962 in the M60 tank and subsequently the M60A1, M60A2, and M60A3, M728 and M728A1 engineer combat vehicles (M60A1 variant), and the Marines' AAVP-7A1 (on which the M85 turret was replaced by a Cadillac Gage Up-Gunned Weapon Station with a .50-cal M2 and 40mm Mk 19 automatic grenade launcher). The over-sophisticated M60A2 ("Starship") used a different cupola with an externally mounted gun with independently stabilized elevation and traverse, and configured for right-hand feed.

However, the M85 encountered feed and reliability problems and was considered too complex. Its 36in barrel sacrificed the range and velocity of the M2's 54in. It required the M15A2 belt link, which was not interchangeable with the M2 machine gun's M9 belt. It also required a different blank adapter, the M20. While many users had no specific complaints about the M85, the Army decided to phase it out. Instead, the M2 gun was to be used on the M1 Abrams tank and other new AFVs. The M85 was phased out of US service in 1997–2000 with the withdrawal of the M60A3 tank and M728 combat engineer vehicle. The M85C was tested as a ground gun with double spade grips, adjustable iron sights, and mounted on the M3 tripod, but was never standardized. The British tested the M85 as the XL17E1 and XL17E2, fitted with special barrels, as ranging guns on tanks.

.50-caliber M85 fixed machine gun

Gun weight	65lb (67lb M85C)
Overall length	54.5in (58in M85C)
Barrel length	36in
Rate of fire	400–500rpm (low)
	1,000–1,100rpm (high)

The General Electric .50-cal GAU-19/A. This three-barrel rotary machine gun is far too heavy to be an effective replacement for the M2. One of the hazards of these high-speed rotary guns is that tiny fragments of the cases are ejected during firing. (Courtesy General Dynamics)

The .50-cal GAU-19/A rotary machine gun was developed in 1982 and introduced in 1983 by General Electric to provide a more potent alternative to the six-barrel 7.62mm M134 rotary Minigun, for fixed and flexible mounting on helicopters. Both of these weapons are electrically operated Gatling-type guns. The GAU-19/A (aka GECAL 50) has three barrels – developmental versions had six, being scaled-up Miniguns, but these were reduced to three to make the weight more manageable. The gun is still quite heavy and requires a substantial mount, making it impractical for ground use; indeed the complete HMMWV weapon station weighs 460lb. Barrel life is 50,000 rounds. Besides helicopter and vehicle use, it has been mounted on water craft. It is operated by a 24-volt DC battery running off the helicopter's or vehicle's electrical system. Gun production was taken over by Lockheed Martin and is now undertaken by General Dynamics Armament and Technical Products. It can be fed by the M9 belt with a de-linker attachment or use a linkless feed. It has seen limited use by the United States on Bell OH-58D Kiowa Warrior scout helicopters and by Colombia (helicopters and fixed-wing aircraft), Mexico (navy helicopters), and Oman (HMMWVs). The GAU-19/A was to have been mounted on the Army's cancelled ARH-70 armed reconnaissance helicopter and the Bell-Boeing MV-22 Osprey vertical takeoff and landing aircraft, but was dropped due to weight limitations.

50-caliber GAU-19/A rotary machine gun

Gun weight	193lb
Overall length	53.9in
Barrel length	36in
Rate of fire	1,000rpm (low)
	2,000rpm (high)
	1,250rpm (HMMWV mount)

Hi-tech problems

The Objective Crew-Served Weapon (OCSW) Program began in the late 1980s. General Dynamics Armament and Technical Products developed the 25mm XM307 Advanced Crew Served Weapon (ACSW) as a replacement for the .50-cal M2 and 40mm Mk 19 Mod 3 automatic grenade launcher. The complete 50lb XM307 (including tripod and day/night sight) was to be transportable by two men. Besides night-vision systems, the weapon was fitted with a laser-ranging system that set the fuze delay of its high-explosive rounds, allowing them to air-burst over targets located behind walls, barriers, in open-topped fighting positions, ditches, gullies, etc., as well as burst inside rooms when fired through windows or other openings. High-explosive antitank (HEAT, a shaped-charge munition) rounds were also provided (incorrectly called "AP" – armor-piercing – by the developer). By changing the barrel and just five parts, the 25 x 59mm (1in caliber) weapon could be converted by the crew to .50-cal in under two minutes.

Development of the HB M2's intended replacement began in 2004 as the .50-cal XM312 Common Close Support Weapon (CSSW), here mounted on a remote weapon station. Owing to its extremely slow rate of fire and other problems the project was cancelled in 2007.

The hybrid gas- and recoil-operated weapon was plagued with developmental problems, and poor project management wasted millions of dollars. Efforts were made to salvage the project by focusing on the remotely operated variant for the Future Combat System AFVs, and little effort was made to develop further the ground version (XM307G). In achieving its light weight objectives, it actually proved to be too flimsy and unreliable, while in addition there were difficulties with the laser-ranging and fuze-setting system.

In the meantime, the Army's M2 and Mk 19 weapons were wearing out from heavy use in Iraq and Afghanistan. Rather than purchase more of these weapons, effort was expended on the .50-cal XM312 Common Close Support Weapon (CCSW), beginning in 2004. This was a .50-cal XM307 lacking the laser-ranging system and using normal sights (although night-vision sights could be mounted). The idea was to develop a rapid replacement for the ageing M2 based on an existing developmental weapon, and later be able to upgrade it to the 25mm XM307G. Weight and bulk reduction were achieved, but the XM312 suffered from the same problems as the XM307, plus had an entirely inadequate 260rpm rate of fire – half that of the M2. With only a 36in barrel, its range suffered despite use of an advanced sight, and if made capable of a reasonable rate of fire the light barrel would quickly overheat. It required the M85 machine gun's M15A2 links, could not use the M2 gun's M9 links, and was almost twice as expensive as the M2. Test firing by troops in 2005 produced much disappointment, and the project was finally dropped in 2007. The Army has therefore continued to procure the ever reliable M2.

.50-caliber XM312 Common Close Support Weapon

Gun weight	43lb
Mount weight	53lb
Overall length	53in
Barrel length	36in
Rate of fire	260rpm

GUN MOUNTS

There are a wide variety of mounts for the .50-cal. Most of these allow both surface and aerial target engagements, but some intended primarily for antiaircraft use have not been as effective when firing horizontally against surface targets, due to mount instability.

The original 1918 water-cooled .50-cal used a scaled-up version of the M1917 tripod (for the M1917 Browning water-cooled .30-cal). A similar, but improved, M1921 tripod was adopted with the M1921 gun. The most common mount, however, is the M3 tripod adopted in 1933, a larger version of the M2 tripod for the M1919 series of Browning .30-cal guns. This is strictly a ground mount, being only 10in above ground; with the legs fully extended it is 13in high. The gun is fitted to a small pintle on which it traverses and elevates, and this fits into a bronze bushing in the tripod's head. The gun is dismounted by a latch, which permits the pintle to be removed and remain attached to the gun. Between the two rear legs is a traversing bar graduated at 5-mils and allowing 400 mils traverse right and left.[6] To this is attached a traverse and elevation (T&E) mechanism that slides on the bar and is attached to the rear underside of the gun's receiver. The T&E allows for fine traversing and elevation adjustments. (Prior to World War II, the T&E device was fitted with a traversing dial, but this was eliminated.) The T&E mechanism can be removed or unlatched from the gun to allow a "free gun" with 360-degree traverse.

The tripod, with the T&E mechanism and gun pintle, weighs 44lb. All three legs have telescoping extensions with locking clamps, allowing the mount to be leveled on rough ground. To be effective, the tripod must be sandbagged in place. If not, during firing the front leg can bounce off the ground, which degrades accuracy. The front leg's normal 60-degree angle can also be adjusted and locked in place. All three legs can be extended full length, and the front leg can be angled steeply to raise the front about 2.5ft high for limited antiaircraft use. For carrying, the tripod's forward leg is folded rearward, the sliding traversing bar is unlatched, and the rear legs folded inward. Set up for firing, the M3 is 71in in length, but when folded for transport and storage it is 41in. Most vehicles with a .50-cal for onboard air defense are also provided with an M3 ground mount.

To enable the M3 tripod to be used as an antiaircraft mount, the M1 elevator cradle was adopted. This was a vertical pedestal fitted in the pintle bushing in the tripod's head. Three stabilizer legs were fitted to the pedestal. The cradle also allowed the gun to be set up to fire over walls, from within trenches, and from behind other elevated cover. It offered a minus 45 degrees depression and a 90-degree elevation. Including the M3 tripod, the assembly weighed 95lb.

When M2s were employed as antiaircraft guns, the 200-round M2 ammunition chest was provided, known as the "tombstone ammo can." It held 100 rounds folded in the lower portion and another 100 in the

---

[6] Mils are an angular measurement with 6,400 mils to a circle. One degree is equal to 17.777 mils.

Vietnam, 1948. Viet Minh fire on a French aircraft using a Browning .50-cal HB M2 machine gun on a jury-rigged antiaircraft mount. Such a mount is of limited use as it lacks sufficient traverse, but a guerrilla force could not afford to be picky about its choice of mount. (Cody Images)

upper portion, wound onto a rotary ratchet assembly. The lower rounds were used first. Empty it weighed 29lb, full 89lb. There was a canvas metallic link belt bag that attached to the gun to catch ejected links.

The standard 100-round ammo can could be used as well and attached to the gun if an ammunition can bracket was provided. In some instances, especially from Vietnam onwards, units fabricated larger ammunition boxes from sheet metal or used larger cans intended for other ammunition.

In the liberated Normandy of summer 1944, two GIs watch over a marriage ceremony in a farm courtyard. They are equipped with an M2HB mounted on the M1 AA extension fitted to an M3 tripod. This 1944 photo shows that the early slotted barrel sleeves were still in use late in the war. A 100-round ammunition can is fitted to the mount bracket. (Conseil Régional de Basse-Normandie/NARA)

The 191lb M1 antiaircraft tripod mount was used with the M1921A1 water-cooled gun. It had a high pedestal with the tripod legs fitted near the top and it lacked a shield. While stable, the mount made it difficult to track passing aircraft, as the gunner was inside the radius of the legs and had to maneuver around them. A tubular shoulder stock was fitted to the weapon.

For the M2 water-cooled .50-cal, a number of ground mounts were available. The M2 antiaircraft mount consisted of a pedestal with three horizontal support legs, allowing the gunner simply to step over them while traversing. The gun was mounted on a cradle and a high-mounted M1 antiaircraft sight was provided. A padded curved back rest was fitted and the gunner stood within its loop, with the small of his back resting against the support. The mount weighed 391lb without the gun. The M2A1 antiaircraft mount was similar, but had much longer legs to provide better stability. It weighed 370lb.

Almost seven decades ago, a sailor mans a .50-cal M2 water-cooled antiaircraft machine gun on board a ship during World War II. But the .50-cal is still used on a number of other vessels particularly for coast defense – a testament to the weapon's longevity. .50-cal guns in this role were largely replaced by 20mm automatic guns in 1943/44. (Wallace Kirkland/Time Life Pictures/Getty Images)

Both the M2 and M2A1 mounts provided a 15-degree depression and 68.75-degree elevation. When the gun was fitted on these mounts, the receiver's back plate with the spade grips and trigger was replaced by a special plate with a lever-type trigger. The gunner aimed the gun by moving the back rest with his body. Two removable 0.25in shields were provided, one on the upper part of the pedestal (this traversed with the gun) and the other fitted on the gun itself. These shields together weighed 118lb. The gun was 49in above the ground and the sights 74in. For semi-permanent installation, the legs were removed and a 52lb pedestal base fitted, which could be bolted to a concrete or timber base.

Although the M2A1 remained in use, an improved antiaircraft mount was developed in 1943. This was known as the M3 antiaircraft (not to be confused with the M3 ground), referred to as the Mk 30 by the Navy. It weighed 380lb with its shield, and 120lb without. This was a more compact mount, with the gun set 37in above the ground. Its three horizontal legs could be removed and mounted in a semi-permanent position on a pedestal base, and it was designed to be more stable and provide more accurate fire than the M2A1. Intended for the M2 water-cooled gun like the M2 mounts, the M3 antiaircraft could accept air-cooled guns as well. (The obsolete M1 mount, similar to the M2, could only accept water-cooled guns.) The trigger control mechanism was a dual curved tubular steel frame, with three pairs of triggers and handgrips fitted to the framework. A plate with the trigger linkage was part of the framework and fitted to the gun's left side. This feature allowed the gunner to fire the gun at extreme elevations, which were minus 15 degrees to plus 90 degrees – straight up. The mount's antiaircraft sights were set even higher than the M2A1's.

There were three similar antiaircraft mounts intended for use on semi-permanent positions on timber or concrete platforms, including watercraft, and they were also used by the Navy. They consisted of a circular steel baseplate, pedestal tube, and four triangular support flanges. The mounting included a carriage, cradle, and large shield. The M39 (Navy Mk 21) mounted a single air-cooled gun, the M43 (also Navy Mk 21) a water-cooled gun, and the M46 (Navy Mk 22) twin water-cooled guns. The M39 and M43 weighed 725lb and the M46 was 825lb. Their elevation was minus 10 degrees to plus 80 degrees. Rather than using a counterweight, they used equilibrator springs to hold the gun stable.

The M63 (T91E3) or "Kochevar" (the designer was one John H. Kochevar) antiaircraft mount was standardized in July 1944, but was not fielded until even later in the war. It is still standard to this day. Developed at the request of the Airborne Command, who required a lighter antiaircraft mount, it was also provided to artillery crews, enabling them to ground-mount their prime movers' .50-cals as antiaircraft guns. The M63-mounted gun was intended to be used against ground targets as well, but it proved to be less stable for horizontal fire. It had a short pedestal on four horizontal legs. The spade grips were removed and replaced by tubular vertical extensions, with horizontal grips and trigger connected to a side plate trigger, and these were integral to the mount. Any .50-cal could be mounted on the M63, including AN-M2 and AN-M3 aircraft guns.

THE WATER-COOLED .50-CALIBER M2 MACHINE GUN EXPOSED

Cutaway key

1. Driving spring rod
2. Trigger bar
3. Latch bolt
4. Bolt latch spring
5. Sear
6. Cocking lever
7. Bolt assembly
8. Lever belt feed
9. Extractor switch
10. Extractor-ejector
11. Chamber (cartridge firing)
12. Barrel
13. Water inlet/outlet either side of jacket
14. Barrel

15. Water jacket
16. Water drain
17. Ammunition belt
18. Firing pin
19. Firing pin spring
20. Barrel extension assembly
21. Breech lock
22. Breech lock depressor
23. Accelerator
24. Barrel buffer assembly
25. Latch backplate
26. Backplate buffer tube
27. Trigger
28. Bolt latch release

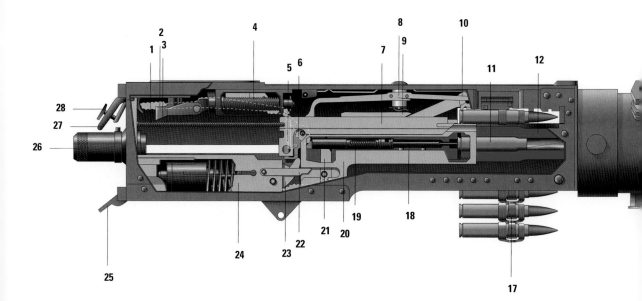

Gun key

1. Front antiaircraft sight assembly
2. Rear antiaircraft sight assembly
3. Belt/link discharge chute
4. 200-round M2 "tombstone" ammunition chest
5. Gunner's backrest

6. Cradle and recoil mechanism
7. M2 antiaircraft mount
8. Water intake hose
9. Water outlet hose
10. 8gal-capacity M3 water chest

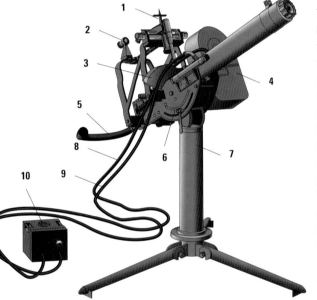

This water-cooled .50-cal M2 Browning is fitted on an M2 antiaircraft mount, of the type used early in World War II. At this time both web and link ammunition belts were in use, and the functional ammunition mix was four ball to one tracer, two armor-piercing, two incendiary, and one tracer, which was excellent for antiaircraft use. It required a three-man crew – the gunner, assistant gunner, and water chest operator.

On Pacific island beachheads the guns were often set up (or dug in) on the open beaches, well above the high-tide line. The guns thus had a field of fire that was open skyward, and which also allowed them to engage surface targets approaching the beach. This was a standard means of deploying .50-cals in both the antiaircraft and anti-boat roles. On island beachheads the Marine defense battalions were deployed to both protect offloading landing craft from air attacks and to defend against Japanese counter-landings. The .50-cals would make short work of Japanese wooden landing barges and long boats.

These large antiaircraft mounts, while intended for ground mounting, could be set up in truck cargo beds to provide air defense protection to convoys. They performed best when emplaced on a sandbag platform, with the legs weighted by sandbags for stability. Any vehicle mounting a .50-cal, however, would have to halt in order to achieve any degree of accurate fire.

Multiple-gun and vehicle mounts

Two types of trailer mounts were provided from which quad guns could be fired. The M51 multiple machine-gun carriage included the four-wheel M17 trailer (a modification of the M7 power generator trailer) with an M45 powered multiple-gun mount. Fitted with a power generator, the electric motor could elevate and rotate the guns at 60 degrees per second. The guns could be powered by a storage battery for a short time, but for sustained power and to recharge the batteries the auxiliary power generator had to run, and it was almost as loud as a lawnmower engine. The guns were fired by an electric solenoid, but in the event of electric power failure they could be fired manually. The four M2 TT guns could depress minus 10 degrees and elevate plus 90 degrees. The mount included 132lb of armor, and the entire system with ammunition weighed 2,350lb. The gunner sat between the two pairs of guns and was protected frontally by a thin contoured armor shield. Later variants increased the armor.

The M55 multiple machine-gun trailer mount consisted of a quad M45C mount stripped of armor on a light two-wheel M20 trailer. It could be towed by a jeep and was designed to be loaded in a C-47A transport or CG-5A glider. This was the mount later used on Vietnam quad-fifty gun-trucks. Both types of trailers had four jack-stands to stabilize them during firing.

There were three halftrack multiple-gun motor carriages mounting .50-cals in the antiaircraft role. The M15 had a combination M42 mount with a 37mm M1A2 antiaircraft gun and two M2 air-cooled guns. The M15A1 had an M54 combination gun mount with the same guns. M13 and M14 multiple-gun halftracks each mounted an M33 powered Maxson mount with two M2 TT guns. The M13 and M16 halftracks had the M45 quad gun mount. The M13, M15, M15A1, and M16 were mounted on M3 halftracks and the M14 and M17 were on M5 halftracks, which were only produced as Lend-Lease supplies to the Allies. The M16 was used through the Korean War.

There was one other vehicle fitted with the quad M45F mount – the 2½-ton M35A1 cargo truck. This mount was actually an M55 trailer mount with the wheels removed and secured in the cargo bed. Late in World War II, limited use was made of GMC 2½-ton cargo trucks to carry M45 quad mounts. The "meat chopper" was also used in Vietnam as a suppressive fire weapon to defend firebases and escort convoys.

During World War II, there were a wide variety of .50-cal mounts fitted on vehicles, most being specifically designed for given vehicles (*see below*):

A posed Korean War-era crew (no one would lean over firing guns in this manner) manning a quad M45 .50-cal. Note the add-on second layer of armor on the shield. (Cody Images)

Mount	Vehicles
M24 & M24C pedestal mounts	½-ton weapons carrier
M24A2 pedestal mount	¾- & 1½-ton trucks
M31 & M31C pedestal mounts	¼-ton truck (jeep)
M35 & M35C skate mounts*	M3A1 scout car, mortar halftracks, & amtracs
M49 ring mount	halftracks, cargo trucks, & misc. vehicles
M49C ring mount	artillery prime mover high-speed tractors
M66 ring mount	M20 armored car, M4 & M6 high-speed tractors

* Skate mounts were a rail running around the inside of the troop compartment, on which the gun could be moved to different positions.

Other ring mounts were designed for specific cargo and specialized trucks: M32, M36, M37, M37A1-A3, M50, M56, M57, M58, M59, M60, and M61. The allocation of .50-cals to cargo and support trucks (2½-ton up to 12-ton) and "Duck" amphibious trucks, plus combat vehicles, meant that one in four US Army vehicles mounted a .50-cal gun.

.50-caliber ammunition

There is no argument that the Browning machine-gun design is exceptional, but what truly gives the fifty its performance is its cartridge. Officially designated "Cartridge, Caliber .50," (CTG, CAL .50), it is variously known as the .50 Browning, .50 BMG (Browning machine gun), 0.5-inch Browning (British terminology until the 1960s), 12.7 x 99mm (NATO), and "fifty-cal round." The round is actually .511-caliber (12.98mm), and complete rounds are 5.45in (138.4mm) in length overall. The rimless bottlenecked cartridge case is 3.9in (99mm) in length with a 0.804in (20.4mm) rim diameter. Cases are mostly brass and weigh 850 grains, but limited issue and test cases have been made of steel, aluminum, various alloys, and even plastic. The non-brass cartridges have seldom been effective owing to production, feed, or corrosion problems.

Bullet lengths vary by type, but the M33 ball, for example, is 2.31in (58.7mm) long, and 1.5in (39.4mm) of any type of bullet extends from the case mouth. The pointed bullets may have a "flat" base (with the edge rounded) or a tapered boat-tail base. Most bullets are typically gilding metal (copper alloy, comprising 95 percent copper and 5 percent zinc) or gilding metal-clad steel, which appears brass-colored, with a cannelure (knuckled groove) in which the case mouth is crimped. Some types of bullets have a second cannelure, used for identification during production before painting the tips. Bullets weigh anywhere from 512 to 718 grains; an M2 AP bullet weights about the same as eight US quarter-dollar coins (700 grains).

The propellant charge can be a single-base nitrocellulose or double-base nitrocellulose-nitroglycerin weighing 230–252 grains. Only single-base propellant was used in World War II. The load disparity means that the different weight of bullets are ballistically more closely matched. The M2 ball is ballistically matched with the M2 AP (2,810fps), as are the M33 ball, M17 (PI) tracer, M8 API, M20 API-T, and Mk 211 API (2,910 fps). The saboted light armor penetrator (SLAP) rounds reach 4,000fps. Most rounds produce a chamber pressure of about 54,920psi. The maximum possible range of a .50-cal bullet is approximately 7,200yds, but the maximum effective range is about 1,970yds. Realistically, point targets can be effectively engaged at 1,100yds under ideal conditions.

Various special-purpose rounds are available for the .50-cal weapons, but most rounds have a lead-antimony point filler for weight and balance (antimony also hardens lead to improve penetration and reduce bullet break-up) and a bullet-shaped mild steel core (slug), making them technically "semi-armor-piercing." (The M33 ball's 380-grain bullet-shaped core is 0.39in/10mm in diameter, 1.85in/47mm long.) Some cores are sleeved in a lead envelope. The base either has a lead filler (if the core does not extend back to the base) or contains tracer and igniter compositions. Some tracer elements are set in the base of the steel core. Incendiary bullets have an incendiary composition in the nose, ignited by the friction of impact. The M1 and M23 incendiaries

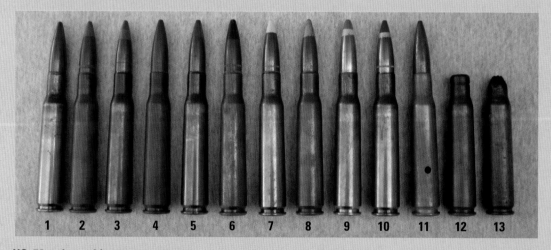

US .50-cal cartridges (left to right):

1. Ball M2 or M33 (no difference externally)
2. Incendiary M1 (light blue tip)
3. Incendiary M23 (dark blue tip, light blue band)
4. Tracer M1 (red tip)
5. Tracer M10 (orange tip)
6. Tracer M17 (brown tip)
7. Dim tracer, experimental (violet tip)
8. API M8 (silver tip)
9. API Mk 211 Mod (green tip, aluminium band)
10. APIT M20 (red tip, aluminium band)
11. Dummy M2 (three holes, tinned steel case)
12. Blank M1 (rolled crimp)
13. Blank M1A1 (star crimp)

(Author's collection)

have inner steel sleeves (hollow cores) containing more compound. AP bullets have either a tungsten-chrome or manganese-molybdenum steel core. Aircraft armorers made pick punches from AP bullet cores. Prior to World War II, AP-T (black, red, green tip) and high-explosive (green or yellow tip) rounds were tested, but never adopted.

Most .50-cal special-purpose bullets are identified by colored tips and some with the addition of a colored band. The cartridges in the image below left are US standard. Rounds with "Mark" designations are Navy proponency, but also used by the Army. Navy designations would properly be followed by "Mod 0" (Mk 211 Mod 0).

Not to be confused with bullet-tip color codes was the World War II practice of dipping bullets in printer's ink, which was for the benefit of aerial gunner trainees practice-firing from ground mounts at vehicle-mounted canvas target panels. The bullet holes would be edged with the ink color to identify the hits by different gunners. The colors were red, light blue, dark blue, green, yellow, purple, and black. Obsolescent ammunition was still issued in combat until expended, or restricted to training in some instances. Deteriorated (non-igniting or early burnout) tracers were also allowed to be used for training.

Other countries use basically the same bullet types and color codes, but there will be differences. A soldier should never assume the color codes of foreign ammunition have the same meaning as they do in the United States. White, green, and yellow tips, alone or in combination, identify many unusual types of bullets, including US experimental rounds. Canada uses an AP-T with black tip and red band. The British have used green for AP, red tip with medium-blue band for dark ignition incendiary-tracer, and yellow tip and red band for ranging-observation-tracer. Israel uses a light-blue tip and black band for the M8 API and light-blue tip, red band, and a second black band for the M20 API-T. The Dominican Republic uses yellow for AP, white tip and red band for AP-T, white or silver for API, and white or silver tip and red band for API-T. Often, yellow-tipped bullets have a high-explosive or observation (flash incendiary) filler and can be dangerous if dropped. US primer annuli are weather sealed with red or clear lacquer or varnish. Some countries have used different color annulus lacquer for cartridge identification.

There was another now-obsolete US .50-cal round fired in the M8C spotting rifle mounted on the 106mm M40-series recoilless rifles. It was a shortened version of the Browning machine gun's round with a 3in (76mm) long case. The M48A1 spotter-tracer round (red tip, yellow band) had a white phosphorous marking charge with an exposed stab detonator in the bullet tip and left a red trace (later M48A2 rounds did not require a tip detonator). Caution: if dropped from 3ft or higher the M48 and M48A1 may detonate.

A number of countries have used .50-caliber/12.7mm rounds, but none are interchangeable with the US .50-caliber. The Royal Navy made wide use of a smaller 0.5-inch V/580 round in the Vickers Mk III quad machine gun, the 12.7 x 81mm. The round was developed in the 1920s and also used in the Mk I, II, IV, and V tank machine guns. Japan and Italy used a semi-rimmed version of this round in aircraft machine guns, the 12.7 x 81mmSR. Germany used a 13.2 x 63mmB round in its MG.131 aircraft machine gun from 1940. The Japanese Navy used a 13.2 x 99mm round in the Type 93 (1933) magazine-fed machine gun based on the French Hotchkiss. It armed ships and was used by the Special Naval Landing Forces. Performance-wise these rounds fell short of the .50-cal Browning.

The best known non-US 12.7mm was the Soviet 12.7 x 107mm developed in the mid-1930s and used in the Degtyarev-Shpagina Krupnocalibernyj DShK-38 and DShKM-38/46 machine guns. An even larger .50-cal cartridge was developed by the British for the Vickers Class D machine gun in the mid-1920s. It was never adopted by Britain, but some were purchased by China, Japan, and Siam (Thailand). It fired a 0.5-inch round known as the V/664 or V/690 (depending on bullet weight). This was the 12.7 x 120mmSR, the case being 13mm longer than the Soviet/Russian 12.7 x 107mm and 21mm longer than the US .50-caliber.

ABOVE An Aviation Warfare Systems Operator inspects .50-caliber machine gun rounds in preparation for a live fire exercise. Rounds are inspected for proper seating in the link, cleanliness, damage, and corrosion. This is a standard mix of one M20 API-T and four M8 API. (US Navy/Jayme Pastoric)

Fifth US Army troops in Italy, August 1944, have set up a .50-cal HB M2 on an M24 pedestal mount. Wooden ammunition crates are placed next to the mount to better stabilize it as it is bolted to a wood platform. (Cody Images)

A variety of vehicle mounts are used today, including the M23 mount used on some AFVs (equipped with a spring-loaded equilibrator), M36 ring mount used on trucks, M31C truck pedestal mount, M24A2 cupola mount on M113 series vehicles, M106A1 pedestal mount with an equilibrator, Mk 64 universal gun cradle used on many vehicles, and Mk 76 recoil-absorbing "soft mount." When used on some postwar mounts and some aircraft guns, the M10 charger was fitted on the receiver's left side. This charger consisted of a rectangular box with a U-shaped handle attached to a charging cable.

As well as the M19 cupola for M85 guns on M60-series tanks, there was also an M1 cupola for M48-series tanks and the M13 fitted on the M59 armored personnel carrier, both for M2HB TT guns. Several models of recoil-damping mounts were fitted on flexible aircraft guns to provide for more controllable and accurate firing. These usually had integral spade grips and trigger extensions.

USE

The .50-cal in combat, from the trenches
to the skies

OPERATING THE BROWNING M2

The .50-cal is an extremely versatile weapon and has been used in countless roles thanks in part to the ease with which it is operated. It may be fired in single-shot or automatic mode, with single shots recommended for targets over 1,200yds.

The following is a brief description of how to load a typical .50-cal prior to firing. Insert the double-loop end of the belt into the feedway until the first round is engaged by the belt-holding pawl. (It may be loaded with the feed cover open or closed, but the bolt should always be in the forward position.) For single shots, the bolt-release latch (a button-like latch between the wings of the butterfly trigger) is in the up (unlocked) position. Jerk the retracting slide handle to the rear and then return it to the forward position, and then release the bolt by pressing the bolt-latch release. The gun is now "half-loaded." To complete loading, jerk the retracting handle to the rear a second time and lock it with the lock-latch release. Return the retracting slide handle to the forward position. Press the bolt-latch release. When the bolt runs forward for the second time, the gun is loaded.

The most effective way to pull the retracting handle is by gripping it palm up and jerking it hard straight to the rear. Many female soldiers and some males experience difficulty cocking the gun due to the sheer physical strength that is required. To load in the automatic mode, the bolt-latch release is depressed. Jerk the retracting slide handle to the rear and release it twice. The bolt will run forward the second time and the gun is loaded.

43

While the M2 can be operated by one man, the ideal crew is four men: the squad or crew leader, gunner, assistant gunner, and ammunition bearer. The gun can be carried by two men while assembled on the M3 tripod, with one on either side of the gun with each holding a rear tripod leg and both holding the front leg. A better option, however, is to use three men, one behind the gun holding both rear legs and one on either side, both holding the barrel changing handle (hot barrel) or both holding the front leg (cold barrel). When the crew has to move the weapon any distance, the gun, tripod and accessories can be broken down. The squad leader carries the binoculars, compass, and a box of ammunition (totaling 38lb); the gunner carries the receiver, T&E mechanism, and headspace and timing gauge (64lb); the assistant gunner carries the tripod (40lb); and the ammunition bearer takes the barrel and an ammunition can (59lb).

Water-cooled guns required a minimum three-man crew: gunner, ammunition handler to change the 200-round cans, and water-chest operator. The latter cranked the circulation handle and ensured that the two hoses did not entangle the other crew or the mount as the gun was traversed.

To unload the M2 weapons, the gunner ensures that the weapon is in the single-shot mode, and then lifts the cover; the assistant gunner removes the ammunition belt from the feedway. The bolt is then locked to the rear, and the chamber and T-slot are examined to ensure that they are not holding rounds. In darkness, this procedure is done simply by touch.

Various stoppages can interrupt the cycle of operation, and include failure to feed, chamber, lock, fire, unlock, extract, eject, or cock. Unless there is damage to a particular component, the failure is normally corrected by undertaking immediate action drill. This involves the following:

A Chief Master-at-Arms clears a .50-cal HB M2 machine gun on an M3 tripod mount during a bomb threat drill in Portsmouth, VA. The .50-cal is extremely capable of halting a civilian vehicle delivering a command-detonated bomb. (US Navy/Robert M. Schalk)

- When the gun fails to function wait five seconds; a hangfire may be causing the misfire.
- Pull the bolt to the rear (check for proper cartridge ejection and belt feed), release it, re-lay on the target, and attempt to fire.
- If the bolt-latch release and trigger are depressed at the same time, the bolt goes forward and the weapon should fire automatically.
- If the gun again fails to fire, wait five seconds, pull the bolt to the rear (engage with bolt latch if applicable), and return the retracting slide handle to its forward position.
- Open the cover and remove the belted ammunition. Inspect the gun to determine the cause of stoppage.

In practice, gunners typically immediately yank back on the retracting lever and continue to fire. In the event of a runaway gun (i.e., one that fires unstoppably) the assistant gunner forcibly twists the belt to jam it in the feedway. Empty cases are ejected from under the gun and the links out the ejection port to the right.

A gunner's mate tests the barrel alignment of an HB M2 .50-cal machine gun with the "GO-NO GO" headspacing gauge during a joint live-fire exercise at Camp Patriot, Kuwait. The two timing gauges are attached to the other end of the chain. (US Navy/ Joseph Krypel)

Much is made of setting the gun's headspace and timing. The headspace is checked and set before firing, after assembling the gun, and after replacing the barrel or receiver group. The bar-like headspace gauge is attached to two flat timing gauges (minimum and maximum) by a small chain. Because the cartridge is held by the bolt's T-slot, headspace is measured as the distance between the rear of the barrel and the face of the bolt, when the recoiling parts are forward and there is positive contact between the breech lock recess in the bolt and the lock in the barrel extensions.

Under combat conditions, or when headspace and timing gauges are not available, "field" techniques can be used. Setting headspacing involves raising the cover and retracting the bolt until the barrel-locking spring lug is centered in the 0.4in hole on the right side of the receiver. The bolt is then held in this position and the barrel screwed fully into the barrel extension; then the barrel is unscrewed in two clicks. Another quick method, although only permitted in combat, is to run the headspace in five clicks, hit the charging handle, and then back the barrel out until it fires and back it out one more click for safety.

To set the timing without gauges, a dog-tag or dime can be used as a fire gauge and a nickel (5 cents) and a dime (10 cents) or four dog tags can all be used as no-fire gauges. Then the weapon is loaded and fired. If it fires sluggishly, the weapon is cleared and the barrel then unscrewed one more click. The procedure is repeated if fire is still sluggish, but never to the extent that it exceeds two more clicks.

A barrel-changing handle is attached to the barrel. While it can be used to hand-carry the gun, its main function is to aid in changing a hot barrel.

Falklands, 1982. A .50-cal L1A1 machine gun is deployed for antiaircraft use on an M63 mount as British troops disembark. "L1A1" is simply the British designation for the HB M2, with the post-World War II British "L" designation representing "Land Service." (Cody Images)

An insulated glove is provided, but an experienced gunner can change the barrel without it. After changing the barrel, the gun needs to be bore-sighted to align the sights with the bullet's point of impact. The gun is usually zeroed at 1,000yds by adjusting the windage and elevation on the rear sight while firing at a standard machine-gun target at 10m range. Aircraft with fixed wing and nose guns usually bore-sighted the guns to converge at a specific range. There was no standard for this range – individual squadrons determined what was most effective for the types of missions they flew, the nature of their typical targets, and the terrain. Most forward-firing guns were mounted outside the propeller arc, thus alleviating the need for synchronized guns, which had a reduced rate of fire. Later Douglas A-26B Invader attack aircraft had eight .50-cals in the nose and three in each wing, plus top and belly twin-gun remote-controlled turrets. Up to four .50-cals could be fitted in under-wing twin-gun pods and a similar pod on either side of the nose, called "cheek guns." These could be mounted on B-25 Mitchell bombers as well.

By repositioning eight internal components, the gun can be switched to right-hand feed. Standard guns are left-hand feed unless accommodated on certain gun mounts, such as the Maxson mounts, aircraft twin-gun turrets, and wing installations.

Firing the .50-cal

Firing a .50-cal is a different experience from that of most other machine guns. When the first round is fired, the extremely heavy bolt slams forward quite noticeably. There is significant recoil, especially since most historic mounts lacked any recoil-absorbing or recoil-countering mechanism. (Many modern mounts now do have recoil-absorbing capabilities.) The muzzle blast is also heavy, and there is a pronounced muzzle flash (at night this can easily dazzle the gun crew). On an M3 tripod low to the ground, the ground will literally be pulverized and broken loose, creating a great deal of dust if the ground is dry. Even over wet ground prolonged firing will dry out and crumble the ground. With a flexible handheld gun not locked in position, it is virtually impossible to hold it steady on a target on all but the shortest-range targets. Bursts should therefore be short and the gun carefully re-aimed after each burst, not just re-pointed in the general direction and fired. Fire can be sustained indefinitely by firing no more than 40rpm in 5–7-round bursts. Flexible aircraft guns were usually provided with recoil-absorbing mounts for this reason.

Water-cooled guns were provided with the 8gal M3 water chest from 1940. They were connected to the 8qt (36in barrel) or 10qt (45in barrel) water jacket by two 12ft rubber hoses. Water-cooled guns can be fired in short bursts with just the jacket filled, but the water chest was necessary for prolonged high-rate firing (bursts of more than 25 rounds). After prolonged firing, the water continued to be circulated until it cooled. The chest had a crank handle that rotated 35 revolutions per minute. It weighed 74.5lb empty and 139.5lb filled. The earlier version held 6gal and required 60 crank rotations per minute.

This M45 quad .50-cal mount has been removed from its 2½-ton truck and set up in a fire support base. It is providing suppressive fire in support of the 1st Cavalry Division (Airmobile), 1968. (US Army)

WORLD WAR II, 1939–45

The earliest role foreseen for the .50-cal was as an antitank weapon. In the 1920s and early 1930s, tanks possessed very light armor, often less than an inch thick, and little use was made of sloped armor. The .50-cal armor-piercing (AP) rounds could easily penetrate these tanks. Most European armies fielded 7.9mm to 20mm antitank rifles by the late 1930s, and these were their principal infantry "light" antitank weapons. At this point, antitank rifle grenades and bazooka-type weapons were not yet developed. The US opted not to use an antitank rifle, but the .50-cal machine gun instead.[1] While a heavier, bulkier weapon than an antitank rifle, it could literally riddle a tank rather than fire single shots, and increase the chance of hits at longer ranges by firing bursts. It could also be used for other targets, including personnel at long ranges and aircraft. The T21E1 tripod was an attempt to provide a mount ideally suited to both antitank (tracking a moving vehicle and aircraft both require a high mounting) and infantry use, but it lacked the required 360-degree traverse, meaning that in reality it was good for neither of these roles.

Tank development and armor soon overtook the capabilities of the .50-cal in the antitank role, but it was still effective against light armored vehicles such as scout cars, armored cars, and halftracks. Even with improved armor, early 1940s tank treads and road wheels were somewhat vulnerable to .50-cal fire. The M1 AP round could penetrate 0.6in of armor within several hundred yards at less than 20 degrees impact angle.

---

[1] The cavalry tested .50-cal M2HBs as antitank rifles with shoulder stocks, bipods, pistol grips with triggers, and T3 telescopic sights, adding 37lb, but these were too heavy to be practical. They were less effective at tracking a moving tank than the tripod-mounted M2.

In 1937 it was decided that the new infantry battalion weapons company was to have a platoon of four .50-cals, two to a section, one gun per squad (although few units actually received them). A two-gun section was typically to be attached to the two forward rifle companies, with the guns some distance apart but covering the same sector with overlapping fire. In the defense, the guns would cover likely avenues of approach for enemy armor. Several alternative positions might be prepared and then occupied as the armor advanced. There was no emphasis on positioning guns to fire on the more vulnerable sides and rear of tanks.

The use of the .50-cals was hampered by the limitations of the M3 tripod, which was not stable enough for accurate long-range fire and was limited to a 45-degree traverse, the latter factor making it difficult to track rapidly moving targets. In the attack, the guns were positioned well forward to place suppressive fire on enemy positions and engage tanks that might meet the attack. They were moved forward as rapidly as possible to meet a possible counterattack by enemy armor, and gunners were taught to engage the most vulnerable points on enemy tanks. Single shots would be fired until the tank was ranged, so as not to reveal the gun's location. Then a concentrated burst was fired to disable it.

Prior to the actual outbreak of war in 1939, however, it was determined that the .50-cal was inadequate as an antitank weapon and they were removed from the weapons company. The 37mm antitank gun took over the antitank role in 1940 and was supplemented by the bazooka in late 1942. In fact, by this point there were no .50-cals with dedicated crews within any infantry regiments. Instead there was a total of 20 "fifties" mounted on trucks and jeeps in the regimental headquarters, service, antitank, and cannon companies, plus two in each of the three infantry battalion headquarters companies. There was also one in each of the regiment's nine rifle companies, assigned to the weapons platoon headquarters and pedestal-mounted on a jeep (although it appears many units did not even have these). The regiment's 35 guns were intended for air defense and ground defense of rear installations. Unit members manned the guns as a secondary duty.

It was not uncommon for some battalions to form ad hoc crews from support personnel and employ them in frontline positions. This practice was not official doctrine, and it had its limitations owing to the weight and bulk of the gun (128lb for the M2HB gun and M3 tripod, plus a 35lb ammunition can). In this role, each gun was provided with an M5A1 two-wheel hand-drawn cart consisting of a steel bed with 6in-high siderails, weighing 70lb-plus. A .50-cal M2 with barrel removed, M3 tripod, and five ammunition cans could be carried in it, secured by clamped mounting brackets and quick-release web straps. But it could be towed only at a slow speed by a jeep or mule.

A World War II infantry division had 131 .50-cals, in addition to the 105 assigned to its three infantry regiments. These were the primary means of organic air defense. Normal allocation to headquarters, service, and support units was one per four trucks, sometimes less. Each artillery crew had a .50-cal on its prime mover; the gun could be set up on a ground mount for both air and ground defense. Medium tanks, tank destroyers, halftrack personnel carriers, armored cars, light self-propelled howitzers, and tank recovery vehicles also each mounted a .50-cal for air defense and close-in defense. In the Pacific, they were sometimes removed from tanks to prevent the Japanese climbing onto them and turning the gun on accompanying infantry. Other units replaced the .50-cal with a .30-cal as a better close-in antipersonnel weapon.

These guns gave units a limited local self-defense capability against low-flying, low-performance aircraft – according to prevailing doctrine, maximum effective range was 800–900yds – but they were not components of an integrated and coordinated air defense system. Gunners were taught to estimate the lead (the distance they had to fire in front of the aircraft to allow for the aircraft's speed) by various methods. Since training was rudimentary at best, and with few opportunities to practise against aerial targets, the most effective engagement technique was simply for gunners to aim ahead of the aircraft and let it fly into the streams of fire. In today's manuals the aid defense role is barely mentioned.

Halftrack-mounted quad and twin fifties were assigned to self-propelled antiaircraft artillery automatic weapons battalions. Each of the four batteries possessed two platoons with four halftracks, plus two platoons of four 40mm guns, to total 32 twin- or quad-fifties or a mix per battalion. Before the multi-gun halftracks were available, the two .50-cal platoons had only four M2 water-cooled guns on individual ground mounts. Mobile battalions lacked the halftracks and so used quad-fifties on 2½-ton truck-towed M51 four-wheel trailers.

An antiaircraft artillery automatic weapons battalion was typically attached to each division in Europe. With armored divisions, a mixed 40mm and quad-fifty battery was normally attached to each of the two or three combat commands, while in infantry divisions a battery was attached to each of the three infantry regiments, with platoons and sections attached to battalions. They were not always available, though, being much in demand for rear-area air defense. When they were available, they proved to be quite valuable in fast-moving offensives and pursuits.

The use of twin- and quad-fifties, and the individual guns, in the support role was both invaluable and commonplace. As infantry support weapons, .50-cals were usually positioned well forward and used for suppressive fire in support of an attack. In this manner, they fired on known and suspected enemy positions, being especially effective against buildings, field fortifications, walls, bamboo (in the Pacific theater), dense brush, and trees. They were also highly effective for defense against personnel. Beginning with a cool barrel, a continuous 100–150-round burst could be fired, after which the gunner would resume short bursts only. Realistically, however, such a long burst was rarely necessary. A few quick bursts at the source of small-arms fire, for example, usually eliminated the trouble. One .50-cal battery commander reported that, "opposing German machine guns had ceased fire due to stoppages … of manpower."

Offensive and defensive firepower

The guns were typically used to place suppressive fire on wood lines, the outer buildings of villages, hills and ridges, roadside walls, hedgerows, and any other suspected enemy positions. They also reconnoitered by fire, in an effort to force the enemy to return fire and expose their positions. Fifties were ideal weapons for providing covering fire when infantry had to cross wide-open areas, and they also covered assault river crossings and bridge construction, suppressing enemy fire from the far side and driving off air attacks.

Any machine-gun tracer fire has an adverse psychological effect on the recipients, giving the impression of larger volumes of fire than is the reality. Some Allied units deliberately increased the number of tracers in their .30-cal weapons, as this gave the appearance of larger-caliber fire. In balance, tracers also helped the enemy to locate the gun's firing positions, and some wartime units removed them altogether. Yet tracer fire can have a favorable psychological affect on the troops being supported. In one incident, a US quad-fifty battery tasked with providing suppressive fire in support of an infantry attack planned to remove the tracers. Learning of this intention, the infantry requested that they retain the tracers, as they had such a good effect on morale and would further demoralize the enemy. The antiaircraft troops granted their request, deciding it was worth the risk to give the attacking infantry such a morale boost.

Another offensive .50-cal technique was for two multiple-gun halftracks to rush down town streets as fast as possible, firing bursts into each building and each floor (the rounds usually penetrated the walls); when they reached the end of the street, they would swing around and make a return trip doing the same. Seldom did the enemy effectively respond, and they often withdrew. Dismounted infantry would then clear the street with the gun-halftracks covering their advance. It was found that the .50-cal

In March 1945 the 9th Armored Division captured the Remagen Bridge, one of two bridges still spanning the Rhine River. The Germans launched repeated air attacks, some even by Arado Ar 234 jet bombers. M16 quad .50-cals of the 482nd Antiaircraft Artillery Automatic Weapons Battalion helped defend the valuable bridge, allowing three infantry divisions to flood into Germany. (Cody Images)

was very effective when fired down streets and alleys indirectly from a street intersection without exposing the weapon and crew. The rounds ricocheted off the lateral street, sidewalks, and walls to hit the enemy or force them to take cover.

Near Braine, France, one unit was alerted by French partisans to the fact that a trainload of German troops was approaching. An M15 halftrack was hastily dispatched and positioned to cover the rail line. A single 37mm antiaircraft round blew up the locomotive, and then the dual fifties peppered the train, resulting in 25 dead Germans and 130 prisoners, of whom 30 were wounded.

The experiences of the 486th AAA Battalion further demonstrate the employment of multiple-gun halftracks. In Mons, Belgium, some 30 Germans opened fire on an M16 halftrack when ordered to surrender. Less than a minute of .50-cal fire killed 25 of the Germans. Outside of Paderborn, Germany, 300 Waffen-SS troops were firing on a US artillery battalion with Panzerfausts and small arms. Two M16 halftracks shredded the wood line and the surviving Germans immediately surrendered.

Automatic weapons units also protected artillery positions, antiaircraft gun positions, headquarters, supply dumps, lines of communications, and other rear-area installations. Even 40mm and 90mm antiaircraft guns were habitually protected by .50-cals.

With .50-cals mounted on so many AFVs and other vehicles during World War II, it is not surprising that they played such an important role in combat. Often one or more infantrymen would be detailed to ride on tank engine decks to operate the .50-cal and drive off attacking infantry with rifles and grenades. The most decorated American soldier in World War II, future Hollywood film star Audie Murphy, made effective use of a .50-cal according to his Medal of Honor citation. The following action took place on January 26, 1945, near Holtzwihr, France:

Guam, July 1944. US Marines transfer to an LVT-2 amphibious tractor armed with two .50-cal HB M2s. The first assault wave would be delivered in amtracs and their machine guns would open within 200yds of shore and keep up continuous suppressive fire as they rolled ashore to deliver troops to the first available cover. (Cody Images)

Second Lt. Audie Murphy commanded Company B, 15th Infantry, 3d Infantry Division, which was attacked by six tanks and waves of infantry. 2nd Lt. Murphy ordered his men to withdraw to a prepared position in a wood, while he remained forward at his command post and continued to give fire directions to the artillery by telephone. Behind him, to his right, one of our [M36] tank destroyers received a direct hit and began to burn. Its crew withdrew to the woods. 2nd Lt. Murphy continued to direct artillery fire, which killed large numbers of the advancing enemy. With the enemy tanks abreast of his position, 2nd Lt. Murphy climbed on the burning tank destroyer, which was in danger of blowing up at any moment, and employed its .50-caliber machine gun. He was alone and exposed to German fire from three sides, but his deadly fire killed dozens of Germans and caused their infantry attack to waver. The enemy tanks, losing infantry support, began to fall back. For an hour the Germans tried every available weapon to eliminate 2nd Lt. Murphy, but he continued to hold his position and wiped out a squad that was trying to creep up unnoticed on his right flank. Germans reached as close as 10 yards, only to be mowed down by his fire. He received a leg wound, but ignored it and continued his single-handed fight until his ammunition was exhausted. He then made his way back to his company, refused medical attention, and organized the company in a counterattack, which forced the Germans to withdraw. His directing of artillery fire wiped out many of the enemy; he killed or wounded about 50.

From 1939 to 1943, Marine defense battalions, armed with coast defense guns and a variety of antiaircraft weapons, had one or two batteries of 24 .50-cal water-cooled guns. Besides air defense, the fifties were used for beach defense, being extremely effective against landing boats. During the Japanese landings on Wake Island in December 1941, 18 .50-cal and 30 .30-cal water-cooled machine guns manned by 400 Marines caused most of the 280 dead and 330 wounded among the 1,000-man Japanese landing force. During the 1941–42 defensive battles in the Philippines, fifties were commonly removed from destroyed aircraft, fitted with crude ground mounts, and employed by the US infantry and local guerrillas. By 1944, the fifties were phased out in preference for 20mm guns, although antiaircraft batteries retained some fifties for close-in defense.

In February 1943, a small 1st Cavalry Division force landed on Los Negros Island in the Admiralties. Surprising the Japanese, they initially seized too large an area to defend through the night. Pulling back to the island's airfield, they dug in on its perimeter to hold off the Japanese. Reinforcements would not arrive for two days so the 673d Antiaircraft Machine Gun Battery set up their M2 water-cooled guns on the perimeter to engage both ground and air targets. The 168th AAA Battalion also established similar .50-cal positions. Their firepower was a significant contribution to the defense, as they mowed down fanatical Japanese charges for two long nights. The enemy made special attempts to knock out the .50-cals and stop the devastation the guns were inflicting upon them but were ultimately unsuccessful.

A .50-cal M2 water-cooled gun set up in a sandbag and coconut log revetted pit to protect a beachhead somewhere in the Pacific. Besides providing air defense these positions were also used to fire on Japanese counter-landing attempts in the beachhead. (Cody Images)

Fifties were little used by the infantry in the Pacific, but were sometimes employed in perimeter defense in those situations where an island was not completely cleared of the enemy. They proved effective against trucks and lightly armored Japanese tanks, and could penetrate the coconut logs and bamboo used in the construction of Japanese bunkers. Antiaircraft machine-gun units were often set up to cover beaches to prevent Japanese counter-landings on US beachheads. As we have seen, .50-cals were also very effective against Japanese landing barges and other small craft, and for this reason US PT boats often added .50-cals and other automatic weapons to their armament. Larger landing craft, such as landing craft, infantry (LCI) vessels, were used to patrol ship anchorages during amphibious operations, and mounted numerous .50-cals to engage suicide boats and swimmers.

In the southwest Pacific, Army amphibious boat and shore regiments would outfit 50ft landing craft, mechanized (LCM) craft with a deck over the cargo compartment, on which they would mount eight twin .50-cal aircraft turrets, usually with the Plexiglas removed owing to the Pacific heat, to create antiaircraft boats to escort landing craft. The 16 machine guns, firing at a combined rate of 8,800–10,400rpm, would throw up devastating fire against fighters making strafing runs.

Bomber .50-cals

US bombers were completely armed with .50-cals: 13 on a B-17G, ten on a B-24J, and 12 on a B-29A, for example. Bombers flew in a formation called a "combat box," consisting of 18–54 aircraft in three-plane "Vs," arranged in staggered and echeloned formations in which each stacked three-plane element provided covering fire to other elements with overlapping fields of fire. Of course, no matter how they were arranged, certain elements were more exposed than others and gunners on some bombers had more restricted fields of fire, depending on the aircraft's position in the formation. Gunners had to be extremely cautious with their fire to avoid hitting other bombers and their own aircraft, as there were no mechanical stops to prevent this occurring.

Maximum range to engage "bandits" was 2,000yds. Gunners were taught "position firing," in which they understood that attacking enemy fighters were aiming ahead of the bomber and not flying directly at it, and were making a "pursuit curve" in order to maintain their lead. The gunners had to aim at the fighter with that in mind. They could not simply lead the fighter (aim in front), as the bomber was moving too – if they led the enemy aircraft the bomber's movement would keep the bullets ahead of the fighter. The gunners also had to understand tracer "cutback." The tracer stream from a traversing gun in a moving bomber gives the impression that the tracers appear to arc in the opposite direction. Instead of aiming by using the tracer stream, they had to use the ring sight to adjust their lead. Fighter pilots attacking such a bomber formation endured a harrowing experience, with scores of fifties spraying tracers at them. One recommendation for Luftwaffe pilots was to line up with their target, shut their eyes, and make their run, hoping for the best.

During training, a 75-round (five-second) burst was the maximum permitted from a cold gun. One minute after the first burst, firing could be resumed at up to one 20-round burst per minute. In combat, of course, higher rates were used, but it was warned that unrestricted 75-round bursts would sooner or later overheat the barrel and could result in stoppages or runaway firing. Spare barrels were not carried aboard aircraft.

.50-caliber M2 flexible aircraft machine guns, B-17E bomber (opposite)

Most of the .50-cals in US heavy bombers were fixed guns mounted in turrets about the ship (top, belly, tail, and in later models, chin turrets). Flexible M2s, however, were used as the two waist guns and the upward-firing gun in the radio-operator's compartment, just forward of the waist position and aft of the bomb bay, and sometimes as two cheek guns in the nose compartment. Waist gunners suffered the highest casualty rates among bomber crewmen. Their guns were initially fitted with 200-round ammunition containers, and later, much larger capacity hull-mounted containers were used. To provide a more accurate and manageable weapon, flexible aircraft "fifties" were fitted with E8 gun mount adapter assemblies and the guns fitted with Edgewater recoil adapters in place of the front trunnion adapter. The E8 adapter was an intermediate assembly that held the gun and adapted it to fit the mount, and included integral spade grips, which were not fitted to the flexible guns. The waist guns had a wide field of fire ranging from aft of the engines to forward of the horizontal tail planes, plus they were capable of extreme depression and elevation. The gunners, however, had to be careful not to fire into their own wings. William Hess, a B-17 waist gunner, reported, "Firing it handheld meant it was hard to steady. You had to lean back off the spade grips as you lined up the ring and post sight. Of course deflection shooting was not easy to master. When a fighter attacked it always seemed unnatural to aim between him and your own plane… the forward speed of your plane was added to the bullets no matter what direction you aimed. This meant that bullets would always strike forward of your point of aim."

Incidentally, perhaps one of the most unusual uses of the .50-cal involved the large numbers recovered by the Germans from hundreds of downed US bombers, along with ammunition. Twin fixed guns removed from American bomber turrets and single flexible guns were fitted with locally fabricated mounting brackets, trigger systems, sights, and 200-round wooden ammunition boxes, and were mounted with pintles on wooden posts sunk in the ground. They were employed for airfield defense against low-level strafing attacks from 1944 and referred to as the 12.7mm Maschinengwehr Fliegerabwehrpivot (12.7mm machine gun air defense pivot [mount]).

Strafing attacks

For fighters equipped with .50-cals, ground strafing was a very different experience to bomber gunnery. Fighters flew relatively low and at a fairly shallow angle when strafing area or column targets, such as scattered troops or vehicle convoys, to spread their fire over as large an area as possible. When attacking point targets, such as gun positions, parked aircraft, or defensive structures, they approached from a steeper angle and from a higher altitude to concentrate their fire on the point. Motion pictures do not do the effects of strafing justice. A P-47 Thunderbolt firing a 30-second burst from its eight .50-cals put out approximately 2,000 rounds, of which about 400 were tracers. The noise of firing was a deep buzz, and individual shots could not be distinguished. It was not lines of spurting dirt that marched across the ground, but virtually an explosion of bullet strikes sprayed almost instantly into the ground or target. Even at 200mph, pilots saw the hellish carnage they created. After long bursts from synchronized guns, the bolt had to be locked to the rear for two minutes to prevent cooked-off rounds from striking the propeller blade. Airflow helped to cool overheated aircraft guns.

As well as ground targets, the .50-cal-armed fighters attacked all manner of small craft, landing barges, coastal freighters, and even destroyers, firing while making steep dives. Dense streams of bullets swept the decks of crew members and frequently detonated ships' ammunition stores, blowing them apart.

THE KOREAN WAR, 1950–53

In Korea from 1951, US rifle companies defending hills and ridges in the outpost line and main line of resistance were typically issued additional automatic weapons. These sometimes included one or two .50-cals. Fifties were more commonly found in the rear either on support vehicles or on ground mounts, and they served to cover roads, trails, and ravines through which the enemy might infiltrate and to defend artillery positions, headquarters, and logistics facilities.

Quad-fifties mounted on halftrack M16 multiple-gun carriages were widely employed in Korea in 14 divisional and non-divisional AAA automatic weapons battalions. Even though jets were coming into wide use at this time, each division had an organic AAA automatic weapons battalion (self-propelled) with four batteries, each with two platoons with four sections having a twin 40mm M19 SP antiaircraft gun and an M16 quad antiaircraft halftrack. These gun systems were of little use against jets, but they soon proved to be extremely valuable weapons. Regardless of the on-paper organization, more often sections were organized with two of the same weapons systems. Air defense artillery had been transferred from the Coast Artillery to the Field Artillery in 1950. Non-divisional AAA battalions used quad-fifties on M51 trailer mounts.

The 32 quad-fifties were attached to forward infantry battalions and also employed for rear-area air defense, especially protecting field artillery and defending division headquarters and airstrips. Some North Korean prop fighters were shot down in the opening phase of the war by quad-fifties. Early in the conflict, the M16s often accompanied task forces to provide fire support, but they lacked sufficient armor and suffered for their involvement. Units learnt to place a tank, with its frontal protection and immunity to light mines, in the lead, while two M16s followed with a second tank behind them. The Chinese would flank attack the lead tank with antitank weapons and the quad-fifties would open fire on their revealed positions. In one instance, a quad-fifty of the 82d AAA Battalion, accompanying an infantry patrol, topped a rise and surprised a North Korean aircraft on the ground accompanied by 200 Chinese troops. The carnage can only be imagined. The M16s were also employed to cover roadblocks. If they were dug in on ridge and hilltop positions, they were especially effective at breaking up daunting Chinese human-wave attacks. Alternative positions were dug along ridgelines, allowing an M16 to back into them so they could be depressed further, plus move quickly to other positions.

An M45 quad .50-cal machine gun mounted aboard an M16A1 halftrack motor-gun carriage in Korea. Multiple firing positions were prepared on defended hills and ridges allowing the halftracks to shift to alternate positions. The "meat choppers" proved to be devastating to infantry assaults and were effective suppressive fire and harassing fire weapons.

Strafing with tracer

A P-47 pilot uses the awesome striking power of his eight .50-cal machine guns to decimate enemy aircraft in a strafing attack. Strafing ranges began at approximately 500 yards. The bullets' tracers would be red, but would appear white in daylight; tracers close to the aircraft would appear as short streaks and then as dots further away. Attacking fighter pilots would dive steeply on to ground targets to increase the element of surprise, while attacking at a low angle ensured that they were able to cover large areas, hitting multiple targets while simultaneously avoiding 20mm and 7.9mm antiaircraft weapons that provided the usual defense for airfields. (Artwork by Jim Laurier)

In 1952, 12 additional M16s were authorized per division. From this year, M16s saw much use as long-range indirect-fire support weapons, engaging area targets at more than 4,000yds. The tracers would be removed from belts of AP and incendiary rounds and adjustments made by the rippling flash of incendiary rounds. Tracers burned out at 2,450yds, and their removal prevented the enemy from seeing the wrath that was about to fall upon them. In Korea, the quad-fifty rightly received such names as "Whispering Death," "Silent Death," "Death in the Dark," as well as the slightly less colorful "Half-inch Howitzers."

M16 halftracks were phased out soon after the Korean War. The Army retained quad-fifty units, though in the form of separate AAA batteries with towed quad M55 trailers and 2½-ton cargo trucks. These were intended for close-in defense of missile sites.

THE VIETNAM WAR, 1963–75

In Vietnam, the US Army employed four .50-cal machine-gun batteries (E/41, G/55, G/65, D/71), which also supported the Marines. A battery consisted of three platoons, each with four two-gun sections. The M45F quad mounts on their M55 trailers with wheels removed were mounted in the back of 2½-ton M35 cargo trucks, with armor added for protection. Each of the 24 gun-trucks was also provided with a 7.62mm M60 machine gun and a 40mm M79 grenade launcher. Sections were typically attached to infantry battalions and mainly employed for firebase defense and convoy escort; they normally could not support field operations unless adjacent to roads. When ground transportation could not reach a remote firebase, the quad mounts were sometimes sling-loaded under CH-47 helicopters and flown into the firebase, where they were set up in sandbagged emplacements.

The gun-trucks could deliver a devastating amount of fire out to half a mile. Quad-fifty trucks were bestowed with nicknames promising vengeance upon the enemy, with titles such as "Bounty Hunter," "Mad Men," "The Butchers," "A Whole Lotta Lead," "Eve of Destruction," "Canned Heat," "The End," and "Meat Chopper" garishly painted on the sides. Quad-fifty gunner (officially automatic weapons crewman, Military Occupation Specialty 13F) training was provided at the Air Defense Artillery School at Ft Bliss, Texas.

This admittedly sloppily built bunker protects Route 19 in Vietnam, 1967. The .50-cal HB M2 is fitted with an M1 flash suppressor. The M1 (T21) suppressor was standardized in November 1944. (Cody Images)

The "sniper machine gun"

Of all the uses of the Browning .50-cal, perhaps the most surprising is as a sniper's weapon. From mid-1951, the Korean War bogged down into defensive operations with both sides making limited attacks to gain or regain ground. Both sides conducted patrols, outpost relief, fortification upgrade and maintenance at night. During the day the hill positions appeared unoccupied, but there would still be movement in the trenches. Lacking dedicated .50-caliber rifles, the US forces set up .50-cal machine guns, retrofitted with M1 sniper rifle telescopes, in positions enfilading key trenches. To improve the chance of hits on daring enemy soldiers, two guns would be sighted to fire single shots simultaneously.

The most famous of the .50-cal snipers, however, would operate in Vietnam. Carlos Hathcock joined the Marines in 1959, after having hunted to provide for his Arkansas family. He won many shooting competitions, including the prestigious Wimbledon Cup in 1965, in which he outshot over 3,000 other marksmen. Deployed to Vietnam with the 4th Marines in 1966, Hathcock was recruited for a new sniper unit program and so began his astounding career. Hathcock's primary weapon was a .30-06 Winchester Model 70 bolt-action rifle fitted with a Unertl 8x telescope, but on occasion he also used a .50-cal HB M2 modified with a Unertl telescope mount of his own design. The gun was fitted with a brand new barrel and a traversing and elevating mechanism to make precise adjustments. The M3 tripod legs were heavily sandbagged in place, allowing for 2,500yd engagements. This ".50-cal sniper gun" was fired from firebase perimeter positions and outposts. On one mission he sighted a boy on a bicycle transporting AK-47s. Declining to shoot the young courier, he hit the moving bicycle's frame. The boy tumbled to the ground, grabbed an assault rifle,

ABOVE: Carlos Hathcock's .50-cal "sniper machine gun."

and began firing it in Hathcock's direction. He regretted having to take down the boy with a second shot.

During his career he was credited with 93 confirmed sniper kills, as well as over 360 unconfirmed kills. Confirmed kills had to be verified by a present officer as well as the sniper's spotter but officers were seldom in attendance on forward-of-the-lines missions. The North Vietnamese issued a $30,000 reward for Hathcock, much higher than other snipers. They referred to him as Lông Trang owing to the white feather he wore on his bush hat. On one occasion he killed an NVA general after taking four days to infiltrate into the area.

Hathcock's sniper career ended during his second tour in 1969 when he suffered 40 per cent burns rescuing seven Marines from a blazing amphibious tractor, an act earning him the Silver Star. He went on to help establish a scout and sniper school at Quantico and remained involved with sniper training until his death in 1999.

A close friend of the author spent two years in Vietnam as a quad-fifty gunner, squad leader, and section leader in Battery G (Machine Gun), 65th Artillery. Serving in the I Corps zone, the battery supported Army and Marine divisions (it never assembled as a unit, with sections scattered all over the I Corps area). On one occasion, a section was transferred from one firebase to another, tagged on to a supply convoy for part of the move, as sections were rotated between bases to give the crews a change of routine. A VC unit unwisely chose to ambush the convoy of a couple of dozen trucks from 150yds. The VC had dug in on a low tree- and brush-covered ridge. When they opened fire with rifles, machine guns, and rocket-propelled grenades (RPGs), the lead quad-fifty halted and the trailing gun-truck pulled up 50yds behind it. They had already begun firing short bursts, but when both gun-trucks were in position they opened up with everything they had, sweeping their fire back and forth along the

length of the ridge and working it over with three or four passes, rattling off repeated 50–100-round bursts. The section leader called for a ceasefire after each truck had expended some 600 rounds. Not a single shot now sounded from the chopped-up ridge. However, no time was taken to reconnoiter it and the gun-trucks rumbled off to rejoin the convoy, which had continued on with negligible damage.

Firebase routine was relatively relaxed. Upon arrival the gun crews first had to prepare several firing positions for each gun-truck, depending on the size and shape of the base and the avenues of approach. The gun-trucks would be at least partly sandbagged in, and a crew bunker built beside the positions. The two primary positions covered the sides of the base most likely to be attacked and their sectors of fire were integrated into the base fire plan. Each truck had a field telephone linked to the command net, and one or two men manned each gun 24 hours a day. Those not on guard continued work on improving their positions, pulled gun and truck maintenance, ate, and rested. Every few evenings, a "mad minute" would be conducted just after sundown. All weapons were fired into their assigned sectors, not necessarily for a full minute, to ensure they were operational and to practice crew drill. The mad minute also served to remind the enemy that an attack would be costly – bands of red .50-cal tracers streaking into the trees, shattering trunks and chopping down branches easily reinforced this impression.

Throughout the Vietnam War, transportation battalions ran countless convoys into remote areas to supply distant Free World bases. Traveling through enemy-controlled territory, they were highly prone to ambushes. To escort and better protect the soft-skin trucks and tractor trailers,

Army of the Republic of Vietnam (South Vietnam) troops man an M2HB on an M3 tripod set up in a little used AA configuration in 1960. (Courtesy of Paxton Williams)

most units also converted 2½-ton M35 and 5-ton M54 cargo trucks to
gun-trucks by adding bottom and side armor and all forms of armament,
especially .50-cals. Mechanized infantry battalions also mounted at least
one .50-cal and other machine guns atop their 40–50 M113A1 armored
personnel carriers (APCs) or "tracks," often backed by M48A3 tanks with
their own fifties. Together these vehicles could lay down a devastating
amount of fire on tree lines and suspected and known enemy positions,
with the dense trees and bush offering little cover to the North Vietnamese
or VC forces.

Some units constructed elevated gun platforms or set .50-cals atop
bunkers in sandbagged positions in areas were there were clear fields of
fire surrounding bases. The guns were often fitted with starlight night-
vision scopes, and the M3 tripods were anchored to heavy plank bases or
steel plates and further sandbagged to hold them stable. With their
starlight scopes accurately zeroed, the guns were used for long-range
sniping to interdict infiltrators and harass mortar men and RPG gunners
out to 1,000yds and beyond.

An unusual .50-cal mounting was developed by the Coast Guard and adopted by the US Navy in the early 1960s. This was an M2 fitted atop the 81mm Mk 2 Mod 1 direct-fire mortar used on various patrol boats and riverine warfare craft. The configuration allowed one station and crew to operate two weapons, an amplification of firepower that was valuable on a small boat. The mortar fired illumination rounds to identify infiltrating boats, which were then engaged with the fifty. The M2s also provided supporting and suppressive fire against shore targets.

POST VIETNAM TO THE PRESENT DAY

Most of the United States' post-Vietnam conflicts, especially those in Grenada (1983), Panama (1989–90), Kuwait/Iraq (1990–91), and Somalia (1992–94), saw US forces employed largely in built-up areas consisting of concrete and cinderblock buildings of heavy construction. While there was little fighting involved, the conflict in Bosnia and Kosovo in the 1990s took US forces into other areas with robustly constructed buildings, while the buildings in Haiti (1994) were less substantial. Heavily constructed buildings and walls are also the norm in Iraq and Afghanistan, where US and NATO forces were deployed from 2001 and 2003 respectively.

The .50-cal – 90 years old and still on the frontline

On March 29, 2005, the widow, son, and daughter of Sergeant First Class Paul R. Smith received the Medal of Honor from President George W. Bush, on behalf of Smith. He was the first soldier to be awarded the medal in the Iraq War and the first to receive one since 1993 in Mogadishu, Somalia.

SFC Smith entered the Army in 1989 and fought in the 1991 Gulf War as a combat engineer and served in Bosnia in 2001. During the 2003 attack on Bagdad, Iraq, his unit – Company B, 11th Engineer Battalion – was attached to the 1st Brigade Combat Team, 3d Infantry Division (Mechanized). During the fight for the Saddam International Airport on April 4, Smith volunteered to set up a temporary prisoner of war holding site when his unit came under attack. Over 100 Republican Guard troops attacked the site with small arms, RPGs and mortar fire. Smith kept his 16 men focused on the fight, allowing an aid station to be evacuated, holding off the superior Iraqi force with rifles, grenades, and AT-4 antitank weapons. A Bradley fighting vehicle arrived to add its fire support, but then inexplicably withdrew.

The engineers did have an M113A3 armored personnel carrier mounting a .50-cal HB M2 machine gun. However, three of the crew, including the gunner, were wounded by RPG-7 and 60mm mortar hits. After pulling the injured men from the damaged vehicle, SFC Smith then manned its .50-cal alone, keeping up a steady rate of fire which

saw 400 rounds fired into the advancing Iraqis. Private Michael Seaman kept Smith supplied with ammunition from within the carrier. Under Smith's covering fire his men mounted a counterattack to drive the Iraqis back, preventing a direct attack on the aid station which sheltered almost a hundred wounded men and medics. Smith had the option of withdrawing his small force, but he chose to hold and fight to protect the aid station. Smith and his men killed 20–50 Iraqis, but Smith himself was killed in the action's final moments by a bullet hit to the head and was posthumously awarded the United States' highest award for gallantry. (Image: SFC Smith, US Army)

Air Force security police heavy weapons specialists fire a Humvee-mounted .50-cal HB M2 machine gun at the Air Mobility Warfare Center, Ft Dix, New Jersey, clearly demonstrating the weapon's brilliant muzzle flash. (US Army)

All these deployments were perfectly suited to the use of the .50-cal. Whether used in urban fighting within remote compounds and tiny villages, or in the mostly forestless hills and mountains of Afghanistan, the .50-cal's range and huge penetrating power have been put to good use. The 7.62mm M240 and 5.56mm M249 machine guns have been mounted on some vehicles, but the .50-cal is generally preferred, along with the 40mm Mk 19 grenade machine gun, because the smaller weapons lack the essential penetration.

In these conflicts, .50-cals have been widely mounted on unarmored and up-armored versions of HMMWVs, in single-gun weapons stations atop the vehicles. In Iraq and Afghanistan, they are also used aboard the new, massive Mine Resistant Ambush Protected (MRAP) vehicles, the

.50-caliber M2HB machine gun "piggybacked" on an 81mm direct-fire mortar (previous pages)

The 81mm Mk 2 Mod 1 direct-fire mortar was mounted on the fantail of fast patrol craft (PCF, or "Swift Boat") and other patrol and riverine craft in Vietnam. Some lacked the .50-cal mounting and were designated the Mk 2 Mod 0. Besides firing high-explosive and smoke rounds, the 81mm was mainly used to fire illumination rounds to light up suspected enemy craft and shore positions. Then the .50-cal would be turned on the illuminated target. The .50-cal was a standard M2HB, but converted to right-hand feed, as the mortar sight was on the left side. The 100-round M2A1 ammo can, as here, or the 200-round M2 ammunition chest, usually held a belt combination of two incendiary, two API, and one API-T, the "fruit salad." The mortar/.50-cal combination was a very effective system, as it allowed two dissimilar weapons to occupy one weapon station and be manned by the same crew, a practical arrangement for cramped, small craft.

Cougar H and HE, BAE Systems RG-33 and RG-33L, and International MaxxPros, of which thousands have been procured. These and most variants of the eight-wheel Stryker combat vehicles have a .50-cal on a remotely controlled mount (see below). Due to the improvised explosive device (IED) and sniper threat, these vehicles' weapons stations are heavily armored. Yet another new use has been found for the venerable .50-cal, with fifties being used to detonate mines – both in combat and during peacetime de-mining operations – and IEDs.

As we have seen, the .50-cal on flexible mounts is difficult to control, which in turn affects accuracy at long ranges. Most of those used in these vehicles, however, have recoil-absorbing mounts. (If more precise fire is needed, various .50-cal sniper rifles are employed, and these are also used to detonate mines or IEDs.) The most effective means of employing the fifty, and other automatic weapons, is to engage targets with multiple weapons from different directions. Once engaged, individual vehicles will maneuver to advantageous positions. In most combat situations in Iraq and Afghanistan the enemy is seldom seen, being dug-in, positioned in ditches, behind walls, and within buildings. Heavy fire is therefore placed on detected and suspected enemy positions, although in modern times reconnaissance by fire is restricted to reduce civilian casualties and collateral damage.

Most variants of the Stryker combat vehicle mount the Norwegian-made stabilized Protector XM151 Remote Weapon Station (RWS). The system allows the gunner 360-degree target acquisition and engagement via a monitor screen. The RWS is fitted with an infra-red sensor, laser rangefinder, and thermal-imaging camera with video recorder. This zoomable camera has a 45-degree field of vision and can be magnified up to 30x.

A US Army soldier uses the Stryker infantry combat vehicle's Remote Weapon System to scan the area for enemy contact during Exercise *Talisman Sabre 2007* in Shoalwater Bay, Australia. The RWS mounts a .50-cal HB M2 atop the vehicle, allowing it to be aimed and fired without exposing a crewman. (US Navy/Sandra M. Palumbo)

An Aviation Ordnanceman mans a .50-cal machine gun during a Force Protection Action watch aboard USS *John C. Stennis*. The gun is fitted with a recoil-absorbing mount adapter. (US Navy/Paul J. Perkins)

The Israelis mount a .50-cal M2 atop the main gun on the Merkava tank, the main AFV of the modern Israeli Defense Force (IDF). Reliant on the main gun for aiming, the M2 is used for point targets beyond the range and penetration of the 7.62mm coaxial gun. For fighting in built-up areas, a specific requirement for the IDF, it is an excellent weapon and is an alternative to the main gun in situations in which the crew need to reduce collateral damage. It is not fired by a crewman lying on the turret, as is rumored, but is actually fired remotely from inside the tank.

Fifty-cals have been mounted on US Navy and Coast Guard small craft and larger ships since before World War II, initially as antiaircraft armament. In recent years, though, they have also become important as antiboat guns to prevent suicide boat attacks and insurgent boardings.

Even though the .50-cal has a maximum effective range of 1,970yds, area targets at much longer ranges – up to 4,900yds – can be engaged by firing ranging bursts on possible target areas and adjusting the fire by observing the dust from bullet strikes. Although it is worth noting that the improved M17 tracer (brown tip) has a 1,600yds burnout. Incendiary, armor-piercing incendiary (API), and armor-piercing incendiary-tracer (API-T) rounds are useful for ranging purposes as they flash upon impact and kick up more dust. The use of binoculars or a spotting telescope greatly aids the adjustment of such long-range fire. Furthermore, indirect-fire table cards are provided in the wooden boxes holding ammunition cans. These firing tables provide the necessary elevation in degrees for different ranges. The gun's elevation can be set by using the T&E mechanism (up to approximately 150 mils), an M2 gunner's quadrant, a plastic map protractor (GTA 5-2-12), or any other angle-measuring device.

IMPACT

The world's most enduring machine gun

The value of the various models of the Browning .50-cal machine gun is indicated by the millions produced and the wide variety of roles in which they have been employed. Prior to World War II, Britain, Germany, Italy, Japan, and the USSR all adopted machine guns of similar caliber, mainly as aircraft or antiaircraft guns. Few were as successful as the .50-cal M2, nor were they used in anywhere near as great numbers. With one exception – the Soviet 12.7mm DShKM-38/46 (also produced as the Chinese Type 57) – none remained in use after the war. Replacement of the DShKM-38/46 by the 12.7mm NSV began in Soviet service in 1971, and in Russia/CIS by the Kord 6P50 in 1998. The Russian 12.7mm guns have remained in use in former communist and client states, while the Browning M2 is seen in service throughout the rest of the world.

Slicing through metal – .50-cal tracer bullets are fired through aircraft armor plate during testing. (Photo by Dmitri Kessel/Time Life Pictures/ Getty Images)

The Browning M2 machine guns have been made in at least nine countries, the ammunition produced in more than 30, and the weapon has been used by at least 60 countries, probably more. Few weapons can rival its record. It is seldom that a weapon design is so effective and efficient that it will survive virtually unchanged for almost 80 years – longer for earlier models – and its ammunition for more than 90 years. Attempts to replace the M2 have been dismal and costly failures. Even though efforts are underway to develop its replacement, the .50-cal M2 will no doubt still be in use somewhere on its hundredth anniversary in 2033.

This longevity is a direct result of the M2's awesome destructive power. A .50-cal bullet strike causes a 3–6ft-high burst of dirt or mud and can spray dirt 20–30ft all around. Secondary fragmentation (gravel, rock chips, wood splinters, bullet fragments) travel several feet. Incendiary bullets shatter on impact with a small bright flash and smoke puff at the base of the spurt of dirt, and generate a little more fragmentation. The considerable penetration effects are the bullet's main attribute, and the ability to penetrate cover materials is crucial. The table below demonstrates the .50-cal's outstanding ability to penetrate certain materials.

Official data – .50-caliber materials penetration

.50-cal armor-piercing M2

Material (inches)	200m (218yds)	600m (656yds)	1,500m (1,640yds)
Armor plate, homogeneous	1	0.7	0.3
Armor plate, face-hardened	0.9	0.5	0.2
Concrete	3	2	1
Sand, dry	14	12	6
Clay, dry (and other soils)	28	27	21

Note: The M8 API and M20 API-T have approximately the same penetration.

.50-cal ball M33

Material (inches)	200m (218yds)	600m (656yds)	1,500m (1,640yds)
Concrete	2	1	1
Sand, dry	14	12	6
Clay, dry (and other soils)	28	27	21

.50-cal ball M33 breaching capabilities (35m/38yds)

Ability to create a man-sized egress (breach) hole or a firing loophole.

Material	Penetration	Rounds required
10in reinforced concrete	12in hole	50
10in reinforced concrete	24in breach hole	100
18in reinforced concrete	7in loophole	140
14in triple brick	8in loophole	15
14in triple brick	26in breach hole	20
12in concrete block w/single brick veneer	10in loophole	25
12in concrete block w/single brick veneer	33in breach hole	45
24in double sandbag wall	initial	5
16in diameter log wall	initial	1
1in (25mm) armor plate	initial	1

A gunner aboard the amphibious transport dock ship USS *Juneau* fires a twin .50-cal HB M2 machine gun during a live fire training exercise. This mount requires that the right gun be reconfigured for right-hand feed. (US Navy/Michael D. Kennedy)

Besides the hardened cores of AP rounds, most other rounds have mild steel cores, including ball, tracer, and incendiary. These too achieve substantial penetration, and any .50-cal bullet penetrating through hard cover materials throws out fragments of smashed materials that cause damage in themselves. The bullets may break up or at least shed their jackets, damaging personnel and equipment with shreds of the jacket, lead, and other fragments as well as the core. This effect is especially destructive to aircraft interiors. Moreover, incendiary and tracer rounds can ignite fuel, lubricants, and flammable materials.

.50-CAL MYTHS

Two myths regarding the .50-cal have been perpetuated, one in regards to the gun's legal employment and the other in terms of ammunition interchangeability. There is an old and certainly popular myth that claims it is illegal to use antiaircraft weapons against troops, especially, for some reason, the .50-cal. There is no regulation in the US armed forces that says this is illegal. In fact, every US manual on air defense guns, including for the .50-cal, has/had a section on engaging ground targets. There is absolutely nothing in the Hague Convention of 1907 or other accords even remotely suggesting that it is forbidden. There is a prohibition against firing high-explosive projectiles smaller than 1lb against troops, but this is ignored today by every country.

Some US officers have claimed that .50-cals cannot be used to engage troops, but it is okay to fire on their web gear and individual weapons, i.e., destroying their equipment, which is a sophomoric if not a ludicrous claim. This issue has been thoroughly researched, checking the claim with different Judge Advocate General (JAG) officers and against appropriate regulations, laws of land warfare, etc. Nothing states that it is illegal to use the .50-cal against enemy troops. US armed forces have routinely used the .50-cal against personnel in every conflict from World War II to the present. For example, TM 43-0001-27, *Army Ammunition Data Sheets, Small Caliber Ammunition* (April 1994), states, "Use: Machine Guns, Caliber .50, M2 and M85. The cartridge is intended for use against personnel or unarmored targets."

A Special Warfare Combatant-craft Crewman assigned to Special Boat Team 22 (SBT-22) mans an M2HB .50-cal machine gun while conducting live-fire immediate action drills at the riverine training range at Ft Knox. SBT-22 operates the special operations craft-riverine (SOC-R). (US Navy/Kathryn Whittenberger)

This myth appears to have originated during World War II. In the closing months of the war, when halftrack-mounted twin- or quad-fifties were attached to divisions, they were routinely used against ground targets, including enemy troops. The fifties were therefore expending ammunition and burning out barrels at a high rate. At some staff echelon it was pointed out that if the Germans were able to mount local air attacks against US forces, air defense units might run out of .50-cal ammunition, having expended it on ground targets. This was a valid concern, even though the Luftwaffe appeared to have disappeared from the skies. In some units, officers apparently looking for a way to justify the ammunition conservation order to experienced combat troops (read as practical and cynical) took the easy way out and lied, merely saying it was illegal to use antiaircraft weapons or .50-cal machine guns against personnel.

One of many myths to emerge from the Vietnam War was that the US .50-cal cartridge is interchangeable with the Soviet/Russian 12.7 x 107mm round, even if the latter is commonly called a ".51-caliber" when referring to the Soviet DShKM-38/46 heavy machine gun and its Chinese version, the Type 54.[1] This oft-clamed interchangeability is an assumption based on the 12.7mm being listed as ".511-caliber" in US intelligence publications during the Vietnam War. Actually, both weapons are .511-caliber, but that does not make the rounds interchangeable one way or the other. The true metric bullet diameter for the .50-cal is 12.98mm and the 12.7mm Soviet round is actually 12.95mm. The cartridge case dimensions and shape prevent chambering these rounds in the other's weapon. The .50-cal round can be individually hand-fitted into the 12.7mm chamber, but it will not automatically feed from belts and will jam when the gun attempts to chamber the first round. If it did fire, the case would rupture and fail to extract, as well as possibly damage the weapon. Additionally, the two guns' metallic link belts are of entirely different design and are not interchangeable; they will not work in the other weapon and rounds of one type cannot be seated properly in the other's links. The US gun uses a disintegrating link belt and the Russian a non-disintegrating belt.

The assumption of interchangeability was reinforced by the fact that US/NATO 81mm mortar rounds could be fired in Soviet/Russian 82mm mortars, but not vice versa. In fact, the 81/82mm compatibility is the only ammunition exchangeability between Soviet/Russian and US/NATO rounds.

[1] The 12.7 x 107mm round is also sometimes designated 12.7 x 108mm; the actual case length is 105.95mm.

CONCLUSION

With the failure of the XM312 CCSW in 2007, the Army began searching for a new replacement for the M2 under the Lightweight .50-caliber Machine Gun Program. The prototype XM806 is being developed by General Dynamics, the designer of the failed XM312 and indeed this new gun is a spin-off of the earlier weapon. It is claimed to be 50 percent lighter (40lb, or with a tripod a total of 62lb) and generates 60 percent less recoil than the M2. Yet it is reported that it has only a 250–265rpm rate of fire, with a sustained rate of 40rpm, far too low to be truly effective in a combat situation. It begs the question, why not just use a semi-automatic weapon? Yet, nonetheless, the development contract was let in 2008 and the weapon is supposed to be ready in 2012.

While recoil can no doubt be reduced (although recoil-reducing applications add weight, if not to the gun, then to the mount), it is probably an unrealistic goal to reduce the gun's weight to make it an easily transportable ground weapon while still providing an effective rate of fire of at least 450rpm. The .50-cal cartridge is simply too large and powerful for such a weapon. A 250rpm rate may be suitable for hammering away at light cover to chew holes, but it is inefficient. It is worthless as an antipersonnel weapon and of marginal effectiveness against helicopters, remotely piloted aircraft, and fast-moving vehicles. In order to keep the weight low, then it must also have a light barrel, and if the rate of fire is then upped the barrel would overheat too rapidly. The Army has stated that the XM806 would augment, but not replace, the M2. But at this stage it is probably premature to assume the XM806 will be adopted.

If modern forces want to retain the benefits of the .50-cal cartridge's performance, they must sacrifice light weight. What is the point of giving up most of a proven weapon's benefits by attempting to make it light enough to be man-transportable a short distance, when it is very rarely operated in a fire and maneuver situation on foot, but spends virtually all

Development of the XM806 Lightweight .50-cal Machine Gun Program (LW50MG) began in 2008 and is supposed to be ready by 2012 as a partial replacement for the M2HB. Its 250–265rpm rate of fire is far too low to be effective. (Courtesy General Dynamics)

its time mounted on vehicles, aircraft, and water craft? It is quite possible that an improved .50-cal M2 machine gun, using modern materials and new construction techniques, will be its own replacement. Yet any improvement or substitution must match or surpass the M2's classic, battle-winning design, and this is no easy feat. It is remarkable that two 21st-century programs, with all the benefits of modern technology, have failed to produce an effective replacement for a weapon first developed in the 1930s. As such, one can only assume that the M2 will still be in active service at least somewhere in the world on its hundredth birthday, making it one of the most successful and enduring weapons of modern times.